Creative Ideas For Advent

ROBERT G. DAVIDSON, EDITOR

EDUCATIONAL MINISTRIES, INC.

CREATIVE IDEAS FOR ADVENT
Edited by Robert G. Davidson

EDUCATIONAL MINISTRIES, INC.

CONTENTS

INTRODUCTION

This book has been produced for use as a resource for creative planning of Advent and Christmas programs in the church. The material has been divided into three major sections — ALL CHURCH ADTIVITIES, CHILDREN'S ACTIVITIES, and YOUTH ACTIVITIES. This does not mean that the material placed in one section should be limited to that area of programming. Materials might be drawn from all three sections to create an all church event, for instance, of projects and learning activities for the whole church family on a Sunday afternoon, followed by an all church dinner and a brief Christmas play, concluding with a celebration worship service. The possibilities are infinite of how a church could use the ideas in this book. Use it creatively to plan for a most meaningful Advent season in your church. Present the Good News of Jesus Christ to all ages of your congregation so effectively that the true meaning of Christmas will live forever in their hearts.

All Church Activities

A CHRISTMAS EVE SERVICE
TO REMEMBER

by Colleen Britton

Every year as the Advent Season approaches we ask ourselves "What can we do that is different this year for the Christmas Eve service?" Last year we combined the beauty of a candlelight service with the simplicity of a children's pageant which involved the entire congregation. The result was a service which was so moving for all of us, that we are anxious to do it again this year!

The congregation was asked to bring a small gift to the Christmas Eve service that was marked 'child' or 'adult'. The gifts were delivered to a local convalescent home and children's shelter following the service.

The table and pulpit were moved from the front of the church and in their place was a manger — a real manger filled with straw found in a nearby barn. Off to one side was a table with the Advent wreath on it. On the other side was the podium from which the narrator spoke. A large gold star was hung above the manger.

All the children were in costume — the shepherds even had life-size poster board sheep. Shepherds and angels sat on the front row until their cue. Mary, Joseph, and the wisemen sat in the back — they had to make a long journey.

After the opening prayer and optional anthem by the choir, the service goes as follows with children's cues in italics.

Narrator: (Luke 2:1-7) **In those days a decree went out from Caesar Augustus that all the world should be enrolled. This was the first enrollment, when Quirinius was govenor of Syria.** *Mary and Joseph walk slowly around the sanctuary to the manger.* **And all went to be enrolled, each to his own city. And Joseph also went up from Galilee, from the city of Nazareth, to Judea, to the city of David, which is called Bethlehem, because he was of the house and lineage of David, to be enrolled with Mary, his betrothed, who was with child. And while they were there, the time came for her to be delivered.** *Mary picks up the baby from behind the manger.* **And she gave birth to her first-born son and wrapped him in swaddling cloths, and laid him in a manger, because there was no place for them in the inn.** *Mary, holding the babe sits on small stool by manger. Joseph stands next to her.*

Congregation: Sings "Away in the Manger"

Narrator: (Luke 2:8-14) And in that region there were shepherds *Shepherds stand up and step forward with sheep* out in the fields keeping watch over their flock by night. *One angel stands up and faces shepherds — holds one arm up.* And an angel of the Lord appeared to them, and the glory of the Lord shone around them, and they were filled with fear. And the angel said to them, 'Be not afraid; for behold, I bring you good news of a great joy which will come to all the people; for to you is born this day in the city of David a Savior, who is Christ the Lord. And this will be a sign to you; you will find a babe wrapped in swaddling cloths and lying in a manger.' *All angels stand up and face shepherds.* And suddenly there was with the angel a multitude of the heavenly hosts praising God and saying, *Angels say joyfully "Glory to God in the Highest"* 'GLORY TO GOD IN THE HIGHEST' and on earth peace among men with whom he is pleased!

Congregation: Sings "Hark, the Herald Angels Sing". *After song, angels stand behind manger.*

Narrator: (Luke 2:15-20) When the angels went away from them into heaven, the shepherds said to one another, 'Let us go over to Bethlehem and *Shepherds kneel by manger* see this thing that has happened, which the Lord has made known to us.' And they went with haste, and found Mary and Joseph, and the babe lying in a manger. And when they saw it they made known the saying which had been told them concerning this child; and all who heard it wondered at what the shepherds told them. But Mary kept all these things, pondering them in her heart. And the shepherds returned, glorifying and praising God for all they had heard and seen, as it had been told them.

Mary and Joseph: Place the babe in manger, walk to Advent wreath and light the candles of Hope, Love, Peace, Joy and finally the Christ Candle.

Narrator: (while candles are being lit) The first candle of Hope reminds us of the great Hope which comes to us through the Christ — the hope of eternal life. The second candle, Love, reminds us of the boundless love of God, who sent us His Son that we also may love and live abundantly. The third candle, Peace, is a reminder of the eternal peace — a peace that passes all our understanding — the peace that comes to us through the presence of Jesus Christ in our lives. The fourth candle, Joy, reminds us of the great joy we share with others in fellowship, celebrating the coming of the Christ into the world and into our lives. The last candle, the taller Christ Candle signifies that Jesus the Christ has indeed come into the world and we praise God for his coming.

Mary and Joseph: Light two long tapers from the Christ candle and give them to two of the shepherds saying, "He is the Light of the World!" (Take original place by manger.)

Two Shepherds: Walk down center isle lighting the congregation's candles and saying as you light each one, "He is the Light of the World." Shepherds remain in back of the sanctuary.

Narrator: You are encouraged to keep these candles and light them in your homes as a reminder of the Light that Christ brings into our lives and to the world. We will extinguish them after singing "Silent Night".

Congregation: Sings "Silent Night"

Narrator: (Matthew 2:1-11) Now when Jesus was born in Bethlehem of Judea in the days of Herod the king, behold, wisemen from the East came *Wisemen walk slowly toward manger, finally kneeling and presenting their gifts* to Jerusalem, saying, 'Where is he who has been born king of the Jews? For we have seen his star in the East, and have come to worship him.' When Herod the king heard this, he was troubled, and all Jerusalem with him; and assembling all the chief priests and scribes of the people, he inquired of them where the Christ was to be born. They told him, 'In Bethlehm of Judea; for so it is written by the prophet: 'And you, O Bethlehem, in the land of Judah, are by no means least among the rulers of Judah; for from you shall come a ruler who will govern my people Israel.'

Then Herod summoned the wise men secretly and ascertained from them what time the star appeared; and he sent them to Bethlehem, saying, 'Go and search diligently for the child, and when you have found him bring me word, that I too may come and worship him.' When they had heard the king they went their way; and lo, the star which they had seen in the East went before them, till it came to rest over the place where the child was. When they saw the star, they rejoiced exceedingly with great joy; and going into the house they saw the child with Mary his mother, and they fell down and worshiped him. Then opening their treasures, they offered him gifts, gold and frankincense and myrrh.

Congregation: Sings "O Come All Ye Faithful"

Shepherds: (from back of the sanctuary) "We too have gifts from him. Let us bring them all to the Christ child!" *(Collect gifts from the congregation and present them at the manger.)*

Congregation: Sings "Joy to the World"

Closing Prayer

MERRY CHRISTMAS!

Creating An Advent Worship Collage

by Robert G. Davidson

Advent is a time for pageantry, a time to give concrete form to spiritual concepts. It is a time when feelings become gifts, thoughts become prayers, faith becomes loving action. It is a time when we remember that God became known to us through Jesus.

We give concrete form to these realities in many ways: we prepare creches, we light candles, we give gifts, we dramatize the Christmas narrative. Another way to give form and shape to the Advent season is to build an Advent collage as part of the Advent worship celebration. Using the five worship ideas presented here can add a tangible symbol to the Advent wreath during worship services.

**First Sunday in Advent —
CHRISTMAS IS GIVING**

After lighting the first candle of Advent place a jewelry box near the Advent wreath saying, "Today we place this box on our collage in remembrance of the Wise Men who, according to the Gospel, came from the East in search of the Christ Child, bearing gifts of gold, frankincense, and myrrh. Like them, we remember the Christ Child in the giving of gifts."

**Second Sunday in Advent —
CHRISTMAS IS SERVING**

After lighting the second Advent candle, place some straw near the Advent wreath saying, "Today we remember that Mary and Joseph journeyed to Bethlehem and searched for a place to rest. But there was no room in the inn, and so the Son of God, the one who was sent to serve all mankind, was born in a stable."

Third Sunday in Advent —
CHRISTMAS IS LOVING

After lighting the third Advent candle, place a shepherd's crook near the wreath saying, "On this third Sunday of Advent we remember how the shepherds were filled with wonder at God's great gift. Like them we are yet amazed at God's great love for human kind which we experience in loving relationships with each other."

Fourth Sunday in Advent —
CHRISTMAS IS THE GOOD NEWS

After lighting the fourth Advent candle, place a Bible near the Advent wreath saying, "On this fourth Sunday of Advent we are grateful that the Good News of Jesus Christ has been passed down from generation to generation to us. In his teachings we find guidance, support, enlightenment, and strength for our daily living. In him we become new persons, filled with hope and anticipation, filled with new energy to go out to meet the demands of a hurting world."

Christmas Eve or Christmas Day —
CHRISTMAS IS LIGHT

Have someone place a large candle on the collage and after lighting it, say "A light has come into the world and that light is Jesus Chrlist. He has shown us a way to live our lives with new hope, new possibilities, and new responsibilities for a future with promise. We are here to celebrate his birth and to celebrate the Good News of God he brings to us anew."

A Christmas Program

by Shirley P. Waite

(The setting can be simply arranged on any platform, or on the rostrum in the sanctuary. Props are two living room-type chairs for Mother and Father, a small table with an Advent wreath on it, and a basket for the family's collection of Christmas cards. Son and Daughter may sit on the floor near the parents. If a Christmas tree is available, it makes a nice background.)

MOTHER: Christmas Eve! It doesn't seem possible!

DAUGHTER: I thought it would never arrive!

SON: : I don't think tomorrow will ever get here!

FATHER: Time seems to go fast when we're busy! But sometimes it seems to stand still, doesn't it?

DAUGHTER: What do you like best about Christmas, Mother?

MOTHER: Oh, everything, I guess! The joy, the gaiety, the excitement ...

SON: (interrupting) The presents, the food, the school vacation ...

FATHER: (laughing) Yes, we like all those things. But just think, if it hadn't been for God's present to us, we wouldn't even have a Christmas!

DAUGHTER: There's a different feeling in the air at Christmas-time, with the music and bells ringing ...

SON: (holding up paper bell) Here's one bell that doesn't ring!

MOTHER: Bells have always been rung for special occasions in the church, and they are traditional at Christmas in many countries. When the tower bells ring in Holland, it's a signal for the children to put their wooden shoes by the fireplace or on the window sills. In America many churches now have handbell choirs. The most famous are the Beacon Hill Bell Ringers of Boston, who give a special performance each Christmas Eve. (She pauses.) I remember when you were just three years old, Son, and rang a bell at the Christmas program.

(Lights dim on family. Nursery-age children come forward, ringing small bells and singing a bell song.)

MOTHER: One of the highlights of the whole season is putting up the Nativity scene and trying to capture something of that first Christmas.

DAUGHTER: I wonder who set up the first manger scene. Do you know, Dad?

FATHER: If I remember correctly, it was St. Francis of Assisi. He had been on a pilgrimage to the Holy Land. One evening in 1223 after his return to Italy, he stood outside the cloister in which he lived and watched some shepherds and flocks in the valley. He thought of Bethlehem and the night Jesus was born. Shortly afterwards he found a grotto and planned a re-enactment of that first Christmas, using townspeople and animals. There was even a real knight on horseback to represent a Wise Man. The villagers agreed to make such a Nativity scene each year to renew in their hearts the love that came down to earth among people like themselves.

(Lights dim on family. Kindergartners come forward, set up small creche, and sing "Away in a Manger.")

SON: I think one of the best parts of Christmas is the tree. Didn't Martin Luther bring one home from the woods for his family a long time ago?

MOTHER: Yes, over four hundred years ago. Luther was walking in the woods when he saw a stately pine stretching skyward, the stars seeming to hang from its branches. So he brought it home, and the family decorated it with candles to represent the stars.

SON: How did it get to our country?

FATHER: The Christmas tree went from Germany to England. Prince Albert carried the custom from Germany to Windsor Castle in 1841, because he knew the children would love it. Ten years later, a Cleveland minister put up the first tree in our country. And do you know, he was accused of sacrilege and idolatry? But a child whispered, "Mother, the pastor's got a tree from Heaven!"

DAUGHTER: Did you know there is a legend about the Christmas tree too? I found it written on the back of one of the Christmas cards we just got. May I read it to you?

(Family nods. Daughter reaches into the basket of Christmas cards, opens one up, and reads the following, which can be typed and put inside a card.)

"There is an interesting legend about how the Christmas tree became such an important part of Christmas. It comes from the early days of Christianity in England.

"A monk named Wilfred was helping spread Christianity among the Druid people. One day, surrounded by a group of his converts, Wilfred struck down a huge oak tree, which in the Druid religion was an object of worship. As the oak tree fell to the earth it split into four pieces, and from its center grew a young fir tree, pointing a green spire toward the sky. The crowd gazed in amazement.

"Wilfred let his axe drop and spoke, 'This little tree shall be your holy tree tonight. It is the wood of peace, for your houses are built of fir. It is the sign of an endless life, for its leaves are evergreen. See how it points toward the heavens. Let this be called the tree of the Christ Child. Gather about it, not in the wilderness, but in your homes. There it will be surrounded with loving gifts and rites of kindness.'

"And that is why the fir tree is one of the loveliest symbols of Christmas."

(First and second grades come forward with a small tree on a stand. They decorate it simply -- perhaps with paper decorations --and sing "O Christmas Tree".)

MOTHER: Speaking of cards, that's part of the Christmas fun, and it starts right after the first of December.

FATHER: Yes, I enjoy coming home from work and reading mail other than bills.

SON: Hey, I can tell you about the beginning of Christmas cards. We talked about it in school this week.

MOTHER: Tell us, Son.

SON: Well, the earliest one anybody knows about was printed from a woodcut about 1450 in Germany. It shows the Christ Child standing in the bow of a ship. Angels are the crew, and the Mother Mary is seated at the mast.

FATHER: Well, that is certainly different.

SON: Sending cards goes back even further, though: the Chinese used to send out New Year cards. But the first published Christmas card anybody knows about was in London in 1843. A man named John Horsley, who was a painter and illustrator, designed it. It wasn't long before the idea caught on. The first one in America was sent out by the Pease Variety Store.

DAUGHTER: Cards have everything on them from dogs and cats to Santas and sleighs.

MOTHER: I still like those depicting the first Christmas the best, don't you?

(Third and fourth grades come out carrying large Nativity pictures or card depicting the first Christmas, and sing, "O Come All Ye Faithful.")

DAUGHTER: I love the candles at Christmas. They add such a warm glow to everything. (Hugs her knees.)

SON: Kind of practical too, with the energy crisis. I wonder how candles got connected with Christmas.

FATHER: Well, the Bible calls Jesus "the light of the world," and we light our candles to honor him.

DAUGHTER: I heard that the early Christians lighted candles as a symbol of spiritual comfort when they huddled in the catacombs.

SON: It didn't hurt to have that light in those dark old caves, either.

MOTHER: Now we have Advent candles, and many churches have candlelight services on Christmas Eve as well. And did you know we have an original American candle?

SON: What's that?

MOTHER: It's the bayberry candle, and it's said to bring good luck. It's lighted on Christmas Eve, and its scent will waft from one sweetheart to the other when they are separated — that is, if they're truly in love.

SON: I think a candle kind of warms you up inside as well as outside.

DAUGHTER: I'll bet the stars looked like hundred of candles lighting the way for those shepherds as they rushed into Bethlehem.

(Fifth and sixth graders come forward with candles. Perhaps one person can carry a lighted one and then light the others. Do whatever is wisest for your situation. The group sings "O Little Town of Bethlehem".)

DAUGHTER: I love the poinsettias at Christmastime.

MOTHER: Say, our Sunday supplement has a very interesting story about poinsettias. Let's see if I can find it. (She rummages through the newspapers and reads from inside a magazine-type supplement.) Oh, yes, here it is.

    "The poinsettia is a tropical flower whose gorgeous red leaves make it very popular for decorations during the Christmas season. It was introduced into our country by Dr. Joel Poinsett in 1835, who first saw it when he was a United States minister to Mexico. Dr. Poinsett, who was from South Carolina, established the plant in his own hothouses, and because of his efforts the poinsettia was named after him. In recent year, white varieties have been developed."

(Lights dim on family. Two adults bring up poinsettias — ideally, a red and a white one — to put on altar or at edges of stage.)

SON: Isn't there a rose called a Christmas rose, Mother?

MOTHER: Yes, and there is legend about it. When Jesus was born in Bethlehem, Wise Men came from the East with gifts of gold, myrrh, and frankincense. A little shepherdess, watching from afar, wept because she had no gift for the Christ Child. As her tears fell to the ground, flowers sprang up. She gathered them and took them to Jesus, kneeling so he could see them When his little hands touched the petals, a delicate pink rose appeared. And so a flower that had never bloomed before came into existence: the Christmas rose. To this day the Christmas rose blooms more abundantly at Christmastime than at any other season.

(Someone — perhaps representing a specific class — brings up a rose to put on the altar or stage. Soloist sings "Lo, How a Rose E'er Blooming" in background.)

SON: Why do they call the songs we sing at Christmas, carols?

FATHER: Well, actually, not all Christmas songs are carols, Son. The ones that church choirs sing are usually hymns. Carols are like folk music. But did you know that originally caroling wasn't singing at all? Centuries ago a carol was a group dance accompanied by a joyful song; gradually it came to mean the song itself, a simple, happy melody that anyone could sing. It still means any song of joy. But more than anything else, it means the beautiful songs everyone sings about the most joyous news people have ever heard!

DAUGHTER: I've heard that the people in Italy who saw the first Nativity scene burst into song at sight, and that was supposed to be the first carol.

MOTHER: So many lovely traditions and legends are connected with this season, but most of the songs we sing are joyful because they tell God's truth: that His Son was born.

(Junior and senior highs come in dressed as carolers, and sing a couple of carols not included elsewhere in this program.)

MOTHER: Let's thank the carolers for that music.

(Father goes through motions of opening a door.)

SPOKESMAN FOR CAROLERS: Sir, we're caroling for (name of church or local agency). Would you like to share with us at this happy season?

FATHER: By all means. We know what a worthy cause this is.

(To Congregation:) Would you join the carolers and our family in giving what you can to support the work of (name of church or agency)?
(Carolers act as ushers, passing their stocking caps — or something similar — down the aisles.)

SON: Say, why don't we drive around and see the Christmas decorations around town?

MOTHER: Fine! Get your coats and hats.

FATHER: (to congregation) Won't you join us in touring the classrooms to see how the children have decorated them? After open house there, meet us back at the dining room for refreshments. Give the children time now to get to their rooms. While they leave, the carolers will lead us in another carol.

(Congregation sings until the chidlren have left.)

Note: The conclusion of this playlet can be adapted to suit the individual congregation. If there is to be no open house or fellowship time, the family can leave the stage after Mother's last line. If there is to be no Christmas offering, Father can ask the carolers to lead the congregation in a few familiar carols. Adapt to your own needs.

Try A Family Advent Wreath

by Dolores Walker

"I want . . . ."
"I hope I get . . . ."
"When can we go see Santa Claus?"
"Do I get a new dress for the Christmas recital?"

Do remarks like these make you wonder how Christmas can possibly be kept as a Holy Day rather than as one long commercial holiday? A family advent wreath can help you emphasize the true nature of Christmas. Perhaps your church uses an advent wreath in the sanctuary. It can also be a meaningful tradition in your home.

You may buy an advent wreath, or easily make one. Just form a wire into a circle about the size of a dinner plate, or use a styrofoam base. Conceal the base with evergreens and add four candles, with a fifth candle in the center. (Modeling clay can be used to anchor the candles.) Some say the first, second, and fourth candles should be purple, the third pink, and the fifth white. This color combination originates in the ancient custom of preparing for a Christian festival by a period of penitence. At one time black candles were used, but purple now symbolizes penance as well as royalty. Pink is the color of joy, and white denotes the purity of Christ. Other advent wreaths hold four white candles, with the center candle being red or purple to signify royalty.

Each week during Advent, one more candle is lighted in a special ceremony. The ritual suggested here is informal and simple, designed with elementary-school-age children in mind. Inside each of us, however, lives a child, and Christmas calls forth that child. So though the designations are "P" for parent and "C" for child, any two or more people can divide the reading and pray and sing together.

Do take time to be certain children understand unfamiliar terms in the text, the scripture, and hymns. Modern versions of the Bible are used for this purpose.

Gather around the piano or organ for the carols, if you can. Or use guitar or autoharp for accompaniment. Or put a record on the stereo and sing along. You don't have (or know) the suggested carols? Substitute other appropriate ones! Remember, this is only a *guide*. Tailor it to fit your family. Only then will it prove a blessing.

If your family includes a John or Joan, you may wish to adopt the European custom of giving that person the honor of lighting the first candle. This is done because John the Baptist was the forerunner of Christ, and John's Gospel begins by calling Christ "the Light of the World."

May your family advent wreath remind you anew of the dark times when prophets dreamed of the coming Redeemer, and when men's hearts glowed with desire for the Messiah. As you celebrate the coming of the Light of the World, may the light of faith be kindled anew in your home.

C: Why are we lighting a candle?

P: We light this candle to represent Hope. Hope is the light at the end of a dark tunnel. The Jews had to wait hundreds and hundreds of years for the Messiah that God had promised. Palestine was a little land, often over-run by foreign armies. The Jews hated being conquered people, but through the hardest times they clung to the hope that someday the Messiah would come to free them. Some scoffed, saying, "After all these years, you still think God will deliver us?" It was a long wait, but Jesus the Messiah did come.

C: I think it's a long wait 'til we can open our Christmas presents!

P: It seems like a long wait, doesn't it? Sometimes we feel like Christmas will *never* arrive. Just as the Jews must have felt that the Messiah would never arrive. But the candle of their hope never went out. Isaiah, a prophet, said the Jews were like people in the dark: *"The people who walked in darkness have seen a great light: Light has dawned upon them. ...Thou hast increased their joy and given them great gladness."* (Isaiah 9:2-4 NEB)

One of our Christmas songs fits very well here. Let's sing **Come, Thou Long-Expected Jesus.**

CLOSING PRAYER:

Dear Heavenly Father: Sometimes we just have to wait. We wait our turn. We wait to grow up. We wait for Christmas to come again. The Jews had to wait for the Messiah. Mary had to wait for baby Jesus to be born.

We do not like to wait. But you help us with our waiting by sending the light of hope, as if to say, "Be patient. It will be worth the wait." Thank you for HOPE. Amen.

SECOND WEEK OF ADVENT

C: Why do we light the second candle?

P: The first candle stands for Hope. The second candle stands for faith.

C: What is faith?

P: The Bible says *"Faith means putting our full confidence in the things we hope for; it means being certain of things we cannot see."* (Hebrews 11:1 J. B. Phillips) The shepherds and wise men had no proof that the little baby lying in the manger was the Messiah. But when the angels sent them to worship him, they went in faith and obeyed. Two thousand years later we share that faith. We too worship that baby and celebrate his birth. When baby Jesus grew to be a man, he said: *"Happy are they who never saw me and yet have found faith."* (John 20:29 NEB) He may have been thinking of us.

SING TOGETHER: **What Child is This?**

CLOSING PRAYER:

Dear Jesus: We believe that you are the Son of God. Yet sometimes we slip into the darkness of doubt. Please keep the light of Faith burning in our hearts. And may we share you, the Light of the World, with all who still stumble in the darkness of sin. Amen.

C: I remember that the first candle (lighting it) stands for Hope, and the second candle (lighting it) is a symbol of Faith. What does the third candle stand for? (lights it)

P: This candle represents Joy.

C: I think Christmas is the happiest time of the whole year!

P: And why do you suppose that is?

C: Because of all the excitement — and presents?

P: Presents are a very important part of Christmas. In giving each other presents, we are copying God, for He gave the whole world a gift on the first Christmas.

C: The baby Jesus!

P: Exactly! God loves us so much that He gives us more gifts than we could possibly pile under the biggest Christmas tree. What others gifts has God given us?

C: (Here let each insert his/her own ideas ... e.g. snow, sunshine, love, etc.)

P: Thinking of these things makes me feel so good I want to tell God thanks! Let's praise God together, using the words of a Psalm:

Make a joyful noise to the Lord, all the earth;
break forth into joyous song and sing praises!
Sing praises to the Lord with the lyre,
with the lyre and the sound of melody!
With trumphets and the sound of the horn
make a joyful noise before the King, the Lord!
(Psalm 98:4-6 RSV)

PRAYER:
(All join hands and raise them high, saying jubilantly: "Thank you, God, for the JOY of this season. Amen!")

SING TOGETHER: **Joy to the World**

FOURTH WEEK OF ADVENT

C: (lighting candles) Hope, Faith, Joy. . .now what?

P: The fourth candle speaks to us of Peace.

C: "Peace on earth, goodwill to men?"

P: Right! That was the message the angels brought on the first Christmas: "...*On earth peace, good will toward men.*" (Luke 2:14 KJV)

C: What happened? We don't have peace on earth.

P: Well. . . we don't, and yet we do. On this earth we still have wars and violence and hatred. But whenever two nations — or even two people — get along, there is a measure of peace. We can have peace in our hearts, and we can live peaceably. When we do this, we help spread peace on earth. Shortly before Jesus left our earth to return to his Father, he promised a special peace to his followers: "*Peace is my parting gift to you, my own peace, such as the world cannot give.*" (John 14:27 NEB)

C: What will we sing today?

P: How about **I Heard the Bells on Christmas Day**?

CLOSING PRAYER:
    Lord Jesus, you are the Prince of Peace. How desperately the world needs the peace you offer. Teach us to live lovingly, to be concerned with all your children. Help us to share generously — not "exchanging presents" but truly bestowing gifts, thus learning the joy of giving. May we be your peaceful people and spread your peace throughout the world. Amen.

CHRISTMAS DAY

C: I know what candle we light today! It's the Christ candle.

P: Yes. We lighted the candles of Hope, Faith, Joy and Peace, and today we light the birthday candle to honor the new-born baby Jesus.

C: But *we are* getting all the presents. Shouldn't Jesus be getting some presents? It's his birthday.

P: I'm sure Jesus would be delighted to get birthday presents today.

C: But what can we give him? He isn't a baby now, that we could give him a rattle. He doesn't even live on earth anymore. So how can we give him presents? And what would he want if we could?

P: Well, now, let's think about that. What was God's greatest gift to us? He gave us himself. And we can give Him *ourselves.*

C: I don't see how.

P: In the Bible, Paul tells how: *"Therefore, my brothers, I implore you ... to offer your very selves to him: a living sacrifice, dedicated and fit for his acceptance, the worship offered by mind and heart."* (Romans 12:1 NEB) In prayer we can offer ourselves to him. Then we do our best to remember that we are his and act in ways that will please him. Since his human body is no longer on earth, we Christians are sometimes called "the body of Christ." That means that we do the good things Jesus would do if he still lived on earth.

C: Like be kind? And spread peace?

P: And joy and faith.

C: That's a good present. Can we give it now?

P: Certainly! Let's pray together: Dear Jesus, your birthday is a happy day. We thank you for giving yourself to us. Now we want to give ourselves to you. Help us to walk in your love and never forget we are yours. Amen.

SING TOGETHER: First, **O Come, Little Children** and then **Happy Birthday, Lord Jesus.**

Christmas Meditation: THE PINE

by Elaine Ward

Three men came riding from the east
Beneath a guiding star,
And sought from Herod at his feast,
For they had traveled far,
To find the whereabouts of him,
The little child of Bethlehem.
They came to find his manger bed,
To honor him with praise.
They did not know the king instead
Would all his armies raise.
They came to bring him gifts of gold,
King Herod sought his head,
But in a dream Joseph was told
And with his family fled.
They heard the soldiers close behind.
"They're coming!" Joseph cried.
"We'll stop to see if we can find
A place where we may hide."
No caves, no rocks, just one small tree
With needles hard and green.
"Dear family, come and stay with me,
So you will not be seen,"
The tree bowed down its branches 'til
They hid the family.
The soldiers passed, for all was still
And Joseph soon could see
That they were safe, thanks to the pine!
"From this day you will wear,"
The infant said, "a strange design,
My hand's imprint to show your care,
And green will be your needles all year long,
And on your boughs the birds' sweet song."

PREPARING THE WAY

by Rudy Thomas

"Little children ask no more,
For love is all they're looking for,
And in a small child's shining eyes
The faith of all the ages lies. . ."

Helen Steiner Rice

There are a few things we do in our church that enable me to see "a small child's shining eyes" as well as I see them each year on the first Sunday of Advent. We are a very family-oriented church and never is that made more visible than during the season of Advent.

Our church has an unusual round Communion Table consisting of a wrought iron super structure with a solid top of one inch plate glass six feet in diameter. Prior to Sunday morning we take fresh evergreen boughs and partially form an advent wreath around the entire circumference of the table. Within the inside circumference of the wreath we place the traditional four purple candles. At the very center is a royal purple velvet cloth on which stands a very large white candle — the Christ Candle — which we use only during Advent, Maundy Thursday, and Easter. The Christ Candle is not lit on any of the four Sundays in Advent, but is kindled at the very opening of the Christmas Eve Family Service.

All of the children, from kindergarten up, are present in the congregation on the first Sunday in Advent for the Mini-Message by the pastor and the completion of the Advent Wreath on the Communion Table. At the appointed time, all the children are invited to come to the Communion Table where I talk to them about the meaning of Advent and then, while the congregation sings the hymn, "Come, Thou Long-Expected Jesus", all of the children help me complete the wreath. Each child is given a small handful of green boughs (maximum length — 12 inches) to place on top of those previously arranged in the form of a wreath. This results in a beautiful creation of an Advent wreath six feet in diameter and standing from ten to twelve inches high. I always have several young people assisting the smallest children with the process of wreath building.

When the wreath is completely formed, and the congregation has finished singing the Advent hymn, I talk to the children about the meaning of the entire setting. The fresh green boughs symbolize new life; the circle reminds us of the unbrokenness of God's love; the purple cloth stands for royalty, the King of Kings; the central white candle stands for purity and Jesus; the four purple candles stand for the four Sundays in Advent. It is our custom to have each of the four candles stand for some particular concept related to the season. One year we named them Wonder, Joy, Hope, and Love; another year: Family, Friends, Fadeless Memories, and Faith. Still another year we said the candles stood for the Wise Men, the Shepherds, the Parents of Jesus (Mary and Joseph) and the Miracle of Birth. Sometimes I specifically name all four of the candles on the first Sunday in Advent, at other times I keep a dimension of mystery in the process by telling the children the meaning of the other three candles will remain a secret until the Sunday we light each additional candle. After explaining about the candles I comment on the significance of the Christ Candle in the center and tell the children we will not light this, the most important candle of all, until Christmas Eve when I hope they will all be with us in a service celebrating the birth of Jesus.

At this point I ask one of the children to light the first candle. It is a good idea to make the selection and practice the procedure with the child ahead of time. One year, instead of a child, I asked one of the oldest members of the church to come forward and light the candle. Another year I had a foreign student, who was living with one of our families for the entire school year under the American Field Service program, light the candle. Immediately following the lighting of the candle I always have one of the children, again pre-selected, offer an Advent prayer.

The Advent wreath remains on the table for the entire Advent season. After several weeks, we replace the dried boughs with fresh greens so that it not only looks good but it is less of a fire hazard. On each succeeding Sunday we have one of our families preside over the lighting of the candle for that day. The candle representing the preceding Sunday is always replaced with a fresh candle before the next service since it is considerably shorter than the others after having burned during the previous worship hour. This candle is lit before the people come to the service.

The family designated for that particular Sunday sits in a front pew. We try to have every member of the family participate regardless of age. One year we had a four-generation family all participating. Immediately after the processional hymn and opening elements of the service, the family gathers around the Communion Table and reads from a prepared script. For example, the father or mother begins with a brief comment about the meaning of the candle(s) of the previous Sunday(s) and the meaning of the specific candle for that day (script provided). The other parent, or an older child, reads an appropriate passage of scripture, after which one of the other children lights the candle for that day. Then follows a prayer by some member of the family.

This ceremony has become so meaningful in our church that I could not do away with it, if I even thought of doing so! It is all climaxed on Christmas Eve when I remind the children of the Advent wreath with its mood of anticipation and expectation for the coming of Jesus as ''the light of the world.''

CHRISTMAS EVE

by Rudy Thomas

It's wonderful to see so many of you here on this beautiful Christmas Eve. Are you excited? What are you excited about? (Allow time for the children to respond.) Do you remember how four weeks ago you helped me build a large Advent wreath on our Communion Table? That was an exciting time, too. It was also a time when we said we were looking forward to Christmas, the time when we celebrate the birth of Jesus. At that time we lit the first of the four advent candles which we said would stand for *expectation*. And now, here we are, full of expectation and excitement because it is Christmas Eve.

A long time ago I read a story that I want to tell you now. I do not know who first told the story but I am sure, like all good stories, it has been told many, many times in many different ways. Tonight I am going to tell it my way.

Once there was a little boy named Bobby. It was Christmas Eve and he was so excited. He had helped decorate the family Christmas tree and had hung his stocking in front of the fireplace. Then he kissed his mother and daddy and went off to bed.

The next thing Bobby knew there was a gruff voice saying, "Get up, Bobby." So Bobby jumped out of bed and ran down the stairs to the living room. But you know, there wasn't any Christmas tree and no Christmas stockings anywhere in the house. Bobby was so disappointed, he almost cried.

Then he heard the factory whistle which he had heard many times and he remembered that the gateman at the factory was a good friend of his. "Mr. Jones will tell me what is wrong," thought Bobby, and he ran out of the house heading for the factory and his good friend. On the way he had to go through the business section of the town and he was surprised to see all the stores were open. He stopped long enough to ask one lady, "Please, oh please, tell my why the stores are open on Christmas Day?" "Christmas, what's that?" said the lady in a mean voice.

Everywhere Bobby asked he got the same answer . . . the hardware store, the dime store, even the bakery. And everyone was so cross, not happy and kind like they should be on Christmas Day.

Just then Bobby heard the church bell ringing. "I'll go ask Rev. Smith; *he'll* tell me what's wrong on this Christmas Day," said Bobby. But when he got to the place he *knew* the church would be, there was only a vacant lot. Now Bobby was very sad and the tears began to flow down his cheek. He could not understand this at all.

Just when he felt so badly, Bobby heard the groan of a wounded man who was lying in the grass where the church was supposed to be. Bobby, yelled, "Help, help, won't someone come here and help this man?" How disappointed Bobby was again when someone said to him very harshly, "Don't touch him. He's not from around here. We know nothing about him. Leave him alone and go on home!"

But Bobby remembered the story Jesus told about a Good Samaritan and so he thought, "I'll run to the hospital and they will send an ambulance." But when Bobby got to the place the hospital was supposed to be, all he found was a sign which read, "IF HE HAD NOT COME."

Well, Bobby was so sad he ran as hard as he could for his home. He remembered last night, Christmas Eve, his father had read from the Bible and he wanted to read the story of the birth of Jesus once more. Can you imagine how he felt when he picked up the book at his house only to find nothing but *empty* pages? There was NO CHRISTMAS STORY in the Bible . . . there was NOTHING, just empty pages!

By now Bobby was completely done in and he threw himself on his bed and just cried and cried. The next thing he knew he heard his mother's voice calling, "Merry Christmas, Bobby, aren't you getting up on Christmas morning?"

Well, you know what? Bobby jumped out of bed, looked out the window and saw the beautiful Christmas wreaths on the doors of the houses across the street. Then the church bells started ringing, as if to say, "Joy to the world, the Lord is come," and Bobby *knew* that all the terrible things he had been through were just a bad dream. So he yelled at the top of his voice, "I'm coming, mother," and started for the stairs. But as he ran through his bedroom door something caused him to stop in his tracks . . .and he whispered, *"You came, you did come. Oh, thank you for coming, Jesus!"*

Well, boys and girls, on this Christmas Eve we want to say just what Bobby said,"Thanks for coming, Jesus." The story reminded us what an unhappy world it would be if Jesus had *not* come. Let us stop right here and do just that as we bow our heads:

Dear God, we have seen what it would be like if Jesus had not come. But he *did* come, and he still comes to our hearts when we welcome him, and so on this beautiful Christmas Eve we say, "Thanks for coming, Jesus." Amen.

ADVENT

by Elaine Ward

Advent means "coming" or "arrival". At Christmas we celebrate the coming of Jesus. The four weeks before Christmas are called the Advent season in the Christian church.

The Advent wreath is one way of reminding us of his "coming," and our preparation for that coming. The Advent wreath has five candles, a white one in the center and four purple candles surrounding it. Each Sunday before Advent one purple candle is lit and so on until Christmas when all of the candles are lit.

The devotional guide can be used individually or in church or for family worship.

FIRST SUNDAY IN ADVENT   ANTICIPATION

Call to Worship:

"Behold, I send my messenger to prepare the way before me, and the Lord whom you seek will suddenly come to his temple; the messenger of the covenant in whom you delight, behold, he is coming, says the Lord of hosts." Malachi 3:1

Lighting the Candle:

We light the first candle in *anticipation* of the coming of the Messiah, Emmanuel, God-with-us.

Bible Reading: Mark 13:33-37

Thought:

As we enter the Advent season we anticipate and wait, watchful lest we miss some of the meaning of this event, God coming among us in the birth of a baby boy in Bethlehem.

The Advent wreath reminds us of God's eternal love, without a beginning, without an end. The candles of the wreath remind us of the biblical story of this love.

Christmas is a time to come inside the mind, the heart,
To meditate, to think and dream, and be apart
From the traffic of the world, its worry, and its weariness,
A time to light a candle in the dark
And feel its gentle glow,
A time to let God bless.

Carols: "Come, Thou Long-Expected Jesus" and "O Come, O Come, Emmanuel"

Prayer:
Dear Lord, "Thou awakest us to delight in praising thee; for thou hast made us thyself and our hearts are restless till they find rest in thee."

Call to Worship:

"There shall come forth a shoot from the stump of Jesse,
and a branch shall grow out of his roots.
And the Spirit of the Lord shall rest upon him,
the spirit of wisdom and understanding,
the spirit of counsel and might,
the spirit of knowledge and the fear of the Lord." Isaiah 11:1-2

Lighting the Candles:

We light the second candle to *announce* the birth of the savior king, as the angel Gabriel announced to Mary, and the angels announced to the shepherds.

Bible Reading: Luke 1:26-35

Thought:

As the angel announced to Mary, *"Hail, O favored one, the Lord is with you!"* the angel announces this same good news to us. *"Do not be afraid, for you have found favor with God."*

As the angel announced to the shepherds, *"Be not afraid; for behold, I bring you good news of great joy which will come to all the people;"* the angel announces this same good news to us today.

Listen and you will hear
The song the angels sing,
"Good news! God is with us now
In *this* happening!

Carols: "Angels We Have Heard on High", "Hark, the Herald Angels Sing" and "Angels, From the Realms of Glory".

Prayer:
Dear God, as the angels sang to announce your good news, the birth of Jesus, we, too, rejoice to sing our praises and our thanks to you for your great love. Amen.

THIRD SUNDAY IN ADVENT   AFFIRMATION

Call to Worship:

"Prepare the way of the Lord,
make his paths straight.
Every valley shall be filled,
and every mountain and hill shall
be brought low,
and the crooked shall be made straight,
and the rough ways shall be made smooth;
and all flesh shall see the salvation
of God."

Lighting the Candles:

We light the third candle in *affirmation* of God's promise of our salvation and our promise to be His holy people.

Bible Reading: Isaiah 62:10-12

Thought:

As God's people looked forward to the coming of the Messiah and their salvation, their wholeness, their freedom from fear into fellowship with God, we, too, wait in anticipation this Advent, affirming God's love in our fellowship of faith, in our families, and in our world.

We affirm the goodness of God's creation, of God's promise, and of God's revelation, his presence among us now.

We affirm and rejoice and give thanks for having been called to be God's holy people, *"the redeemed of the Lord."*

Carols: "O Come, All Ye Faithful", "It Came Upon a Midnight Clear" and "Joy to the World".

Prayer:

"Lord, now lettest thou thy servant depart in peace, according to thy word; for mine eyes have seen thy salvation, which thou hast prepared in the presence of all people; a light for revelation to the Gentiles, and for glory to thy people Israel." Amen. Luke 2:29-32

FOURTH SUNDAY IN ADVENT   ARRIVAL

Call to Worship:

"...the Lord himself will give you a sign. Behold, a young woman shall conceive and bear a son, and shall call his name Immanuel." Isaiah 7:14

Lighting the Candles:

We light the fourth candle in celebration of the *arrival* of the baby, born in a stable at Bethlehem, whose name is Immanuel, God-with-us.

Bible Reading: Luke 2:1-7

Thought:

From home and hearth
And hostel turned away,
They found a simple
Stable and some hay,
A symbol of the way
We still refuse
The needy from our hearts
And homes and pews.

The story of the arrival of Mary and Joseph in Bethlehem reminds us of our refusal to see the needs of the lonely, the sad, the hurt, and the hungry. The story of the arrival, the birth, of Jesus in a simple manger filled with hay reminds us of our priorities at Christmas. This Advent may we change our question, "What do you want for Christmas?" to "How does God speak to you in the arrival of His son?"

Carols: "O Little Town of Bethlehem" and "The First Noel".

Prayer:

"Glory be to the Father, and to the Son, and to the Holy Ghost; as it was in the beginning, is now and shall be world without end. Amen."

CHRISTMAS EVE (OR DAY)   APPRECIATION

Call to Worship:

"For to us a child is born, to us a son is given; And the government will be upon his shoulder, and his name will be called 'Wonderful Counselor, Mighty God, Everlasting Father, Prince of Peace.'" Isaiah 9:6

Lighting the Candles:

We light the Christmas candle in *appreciation* and thanksgiving for God's great love, revealed in the birth of Jesus Christ.

Bible Reading: Luke 2:1-20

Thought:

"And the shepherds returned ..." We have entered Advent with anticipation and at last the day for which we have waited has arrived ... Jesus is born! Like the shepherds, however, soon we must return to the daily routine of our lives and work.

The shepherds returned, however, *"glorifying and praising God for all they had heard and seen, as it had been told them."* We, too, appreciate what we have seen and heard, and glorify and praise God, from whom all happiness, peace, and love have come.

"Praise the Lord!
Praise God in his sanctuary;
praise him in his mighty firmament!
Praise him for his mighty deeds;
praise him according to his exceeding greatness!"
Psalm 150:1-2

Carol: "Away in a Manger" and "Silent Night".

Prayer:

We praise you, we bless you, we glorify you, we give thanks to you for all your gifts, but especially for your gift of Jesus, your only begotten son. Amen.

Celebrations Around the World

by Joan Sinclair

Ireland

Wren Day

On December 26th, St. Stephen's Day, young boys don costumes and occasionally blacken their faces with charcoal as a disguise. They go from house to house with a stuffed wren, or one made of straw, singing about the wren and asking for a 'trate'.

An Irish folktale tells of birds gathering to choose a king. A contest was held to decide which bird could fly the highest. Knowing the eagle would win, the wren climbed on his back and remained there until the eagle had spent his strength. Then the wren flew higher.

Another custom of the Irish is the placing of a lighted candle in the window on Christmas Eve. The candle has long served as a symbol of welcome to Mary and Joseph who sought shelter in vain in Bethlehem. A loaf of bread filled with caraway seeds and raisins is placed on the kitchen table, with a pitcher of milk and a lighted candle. The door is left unlocked so that the Holy Family or any traveler will be able to enter and feel welcome.

Mexico

The Posada

In Mexico the Christmas season lasts from December 16 to January 6. On the first day the members of the family enact the 'Posada' in memory of Mary and Joseph's search for rooms on the first Christmas Eve. They form a procession, led by two children carrying figures of Mary and Joseph, and go from room to room. At each door they beg to enter, but are refused. At last when they reach the room containing the altar, they are admitted. They place the figures of Mary and Joseph in the tiny stable — but they do not put the figure of the infant Jesus in the manger until Christmas Eve.

A social hour follows the 'Posada'. The host invites children into his yard to break the pinata'. This is a brightly decorated papier-mache figure, usually an animal, filled with gifts and candy. It hangs by a cord from the ceiling or tree branch. The children are blindfolded and take turns hitting the 'pinata' with a stick. When it breaks the children scamper around to gather the gifts and candy.

Sweden

Saint Lucia's Day
and Julafton

In Sweden the Christmas season begins on December 13th with the feast of St. Lucia and ends on January 13th. Preparations for the Yule Season begin early in December. The term "Yule" may have come from 'hjul', meaning wheel, which suggests the turning of the seasons. The Yule goat, 'Julbrack', made of straw is a replica of Thor's goat on which the bringer of gifts rides. It also stands ready to butt any child that is disobedient during the Christmas season.

St. Lucia, known as the "Queen of Light", was born in Sicily. On the eve of her marriage, it is told, she gave away her entire dowry to the poor and publicly admitted that she had become a Christian. Another account has it that she also brought food to the hungry people of Sweden during the time of famine. She was dressed in white and a luminous halo encircled her head.

The appearance of the "Queen of Light" at this season symbolizes the return of light after the dark days. Before dawn on December 13, the oldest daughter dons a white robe and places a crown of lighted candles on her head. She goes from room to room inviting her family to breakfast of coffee and 'lussekatter' (Lucia's Cats).**

Another hight point of the holidays comes on Christmas Eve (Julafton). Daily occupations cease and everyone hurries home to the midday meal. The kitchen is bright with colored candlesticks and vases of flowers and pine branches. The family gathers here for the dipping of the bread in the pot simmering on the stove, know as 'doppa i gryton'. It is made with the drippings of pork, sausage and corned beef. Slices of wort bread are speared on forks and dipped into the liquid — in remembrance of the famine when the only food was dark bread and broth. When the dipping is over, luncheon is served.

** Lucia's Cats:
2 cakes yeast
¼ C. warm water
1 C. evaporated milk
2/3 C. sugar
3 large eggs
1 t. salt
1 C. butter, melted
4½ C. flour
1½ C. rolled oats
1 t. saffron

Dissolve yeast in water. Blend evaporated milk, sugar, salt, and melted better. Mix thoroughly. Add yeast mixture, oats, saffron and half the flour. Beat well, then stir in enough flour to make a soft but workable dough. Pour onto floured bread board and knead until smooth. Place in a bowl, brush with butter, cover and let rise until double. Punch down, turn out on board, cover, let stand for 10 minutes. Take a small portion of dough at a time and twist into a rope. Cut ropes into 5-inch strips, each strip about one inch wide. Cross to form an X; turn each end out slightly. Place on buttered cookie sheets and let rise. Decorate with raisins or almonds and brush with butter. Bake at 350 degrees for 15 - 20 minutes.

Jewish

Hanukkah

Hanukkah, or "Feast of Lights", is a Jewish holiday celebrated on December 3rd this year to commemorate the Maccabean struggle for religious freedom. More than 2,000 years ago the Maccabees triumphed over the Syrian King Antiochus who had tried to force paganism upon the Jews. They recaptured Jerusalem and re-dedicated the Holy Temple. In so doing they found only enough oil in the 'Menorah' (candelabra) to last one day. But, miraculously, it burned for eight days.

The holiday is basically a home festival and begins with the lighting of the first candle of the eight-branched 'Menorah'. Hanukkah is celebrated for eight days with the lighting of a candle each successive night until all are burning. The lamp is usually placed on a window sill or some other place where it can be seen from the outside.

It is an especially happy time for children because it is a time for feasting, singing, playing games and exchanging gifts (one each night), and Hanukkah "gelt" (money, mostly gold candy coins) from relatives. A favorite game is the spinning of the 'dreidel'* (a square-sided top inscribed with the Hebrew letters 'Nun', 'Gimel', 'Heh' and 'Shin'), meaning, "A great miracle happened here." To play the dreidel game the children sit at the table on which a cricle, two feet in diameter and a large Hebrew 'Peh' (pot) has been drawn. The players start with an equal number of counters from which each contributes to the pot. The dreidel is spun by each in turn. The letters on the sides of the top indicate a different result of the play. If the dreidel rests with the letter 'Gimel' up, the player wins the entire pot. If it falls with the letter 'Heh' up, the player receives half. If it rests with the letter 'Shin' up, the player has to add a counter to the 'pot'. If it falls with the letter 'Nun' up, the player receives nothing.

A second game is one in which the Hebrew letters stand for their numberical values, i.e., 'Nun' — 50, 'Gimel' — 3, 'Heh' — 5 and 'Shin' — 300. The players agree beforehand upon a certain goal or limit, and the person who is first to reach the limit is declared the winner.

Still another game involves skill in spinning the dreidel. A record is kept of the time in which the spinning dreidel is in motion. The player who spins the top for the longest period of time is the winner.

One of the traditional foods served at this time is called 'latkes', which is a potato pancake fried in oil and garnished with sour cream. The oil is symbolic of the oil in the 'Menorah'.

*To make dreidles for your Hanukkah celebration: Use a sharpened pencil, dot the center of a four-inch square of construction paper. Fold each corner in to meet the center dot. Draw the Hebrew letters: ש א ג ה Insert pencil to spin.

Children's Activities

SANTA'S GIFT

by Janice Bacon

The school bus stopped at the end of their long lane. Jeff and Jenny got off with their school books and small presents the teacher had given them. Their friends shouted "Merry Christmas" — "Happy New Year!" The bus driver closed the door saying, "See you next year!" Jeff and Jenny laughed and said, "Merry Christmas and see you in the Happy New Year!"

The children waved until the red lights on the bus blinked out around a curve. They looked in the mailbox which was empty then raced down the snowy path to their home.

Smoke was coming from the chimney and they could see mother in the kitchen. As they burst through the back door, both trying to get through at once, they shouted, "Merry Christmas, Mom!"

"Merry Christmas to you, too," Mother laughed. "Now get out of those wet things and come hlep me with these popcorn ball."

"All right," they said together and quickly shed mittens, coats and boots. The molasses syrup smelled good and they were starved.

Jeff and Jennifer lived on a farm a long way from town. They had lots of friends at school, but it was too far for them to come out to the farm very often, so Jeff and Jenny enjoyed each other's company and did many things together. They took care of the chickens and ducks and their old pony,

Bonus. The farm was a great place to live and they enjoyed having the meadows and fields to play in. In summer they had a small pond and what they called their very own river for swimming and fishing.

But now it was Christmas — the best time of all. For days mother had been baking and making things. Everyday when the children came home, the kitchen smelled like spicy gingerbread, butter cookies or mother's famous Christmas bread. This was the time, too, when everyone had secrets from everyone else. Mysterious boxes with bright paper and matching ribbons were to be found in every closet and under every bed. It was fun to be preparing for Christmas!

So at last, school was out for the holidays and tomorrow was Christmas Eve! The Christmas tree they had helped cut was up in the living room and it surely was the prettiest one they had ever had. Gingerbread people, decorated cookies and soon popcorn balls would make their tree as good to eat as it was to look at!

On Christmas Eve, the pink fingers of dawn reached across the barnyard and woke "Old Red" the rooster. He, in turn, raised his loud voice to wake everyone else. Soon the barn was alive with the sounds of morning. Jeff and Jenny woke up, too, and jumped up to start their Christmas Eve early. They had to finish wrapping presents and go

with Mom to deliver cookies to friends. They loved seeing the surprised happy looks on the faces of some of the folks they visited.

The best part of the day, though, was the time when Mother helped them set up the creche. It had become their special job to arrange the figures on a small table near the fireplace. The delicate figures had belonged to their great-great grandmother and were very beautiful.

Jeff went to the barn to bring in a handful of fresh straw. Jenny polished the little table and brought in the old family Bible with the gold book mark. When they had everything ready, they began to unwrap the figures carefully. A brown, flop-eared donkey came first. Then two white sheep and a fat cow, much like the one in their own barn. The little stall was set in place and Jeff's straw laid inside. Mary in her blue cloak and solemn Joseph were placed carefully and then, very, very gently, Jeff unwrapped the tiny manger and Jen placed the figure of the babe on a few whisps of straw. It was done except for the Bible. They knew just where to find the Christmas story in Luke, so they turned the pages until they found the words . . ."*and it came to pass in those days that a decree went out from Caesar Augustus that all the world should be enrolled . . .*" Jenny put the Bible next to the creche and laid the gold ribbon book mark in the crease.

More quickly than they thought possible, it was time for bed. Stockings were hung, **The Night Before Christmas** was read and the traditional cookies and milk were set out on the mantle piece. The fire was allowed to go out in the fireplace, because, of course, Santa had to have someway to get into the house! Mother and Dad listened to their prayers and shared their excitement and expectations for Christmas. It was such an exciting night!

Before they settled down, Jeff and Jenny crept out of their beds to look out the window. The moon was not full, but it hung low and clear out over the fields. Its light made a silver path across the snow which seemed to lead right up to their house. The stars were bright and exceptionally close. It really was a magic night. One could feel it!

Sometime late in the night, long after the house was quiet and the children were asleep, something woke them. It was not really a noise. They didn't hear anything that they could be sure of. But something wakened both of them.

"Jeff, are you awake?"

"Yes. Did you hear something?"

"I think so, but I'm not sure.'"

Jenny slipped out of bed and went to the window. The moon was gone now, but the stars were even more brilliant. One especially large one seemed to hang low enough to touch the barn roof.

"Jeff, look!"

Jeff looked out of the window, too, and both of them were very quiet. They sensed a difference in this night but couldn't say what it was.

That same mysterious "something" made them turn away from the window and leave their room. They went downstairs and into the living room. That was strange, they had not left a light burning on the creche table, but there was one there now. What was going on?

Curiosity kept them moving into the room. As they got closer to the creche they heard a deep voice saying, "*And while they were there, the time came for her to be delivered. And she gave birth to*

her first born son and wrapped him in swaddling cloths and laid him in a manger.''

They had never heard that voice before, but something about it attracted Jeff and Jenny. They were not afraid. They walked quietly around the big wing chair and saw the person with the deep kind voice sitting there reading from the old family Bible. He saw the children then and he stopped reading.

"Hello, Jenny and Jeff. I'm glad you came. I've had a busy night but when I got here and saw the beatiful creche and the old Bible turned to the right place, I decided to give myself a present. I wanted to read about the baby and the manger, about Mary and Joseph and the animals. I needed to sit down for a few minutes to remember what Christmas is really all about.''

"Oh, yes," he continued, "I know that my visit is what children think Christmas is all about. And the presents I leave are all they look forward to. But *I* am not the story of Christmas. The greatest gift to all people was the one that was found in that manger all those long years ago. My gifts are supposed to remind people of that . . .but they forget.''

The large man with the funny beard looked very sad. Oh, he looked like he laughed a lot. His eyes were happy eyes and the crinkles on his face looked like they were caused by smiling, but right now, he looked sad and tired.

Jeff and Jenny climbed up into the large lap and snuggled down. The deep kind voice began reading again softly. *"And in that region there were shepherds keeping watch over their flock by night and an angel of the Lord appeared to them and the angel said, 'Be not afraid. For I bring you good news. For unto you this day is born a Saviour which is Christ the Lord' ''.*

When morning came, the children woke from the chill. There they were, snuggled in the big old wing chair next to the creche table in the living room. The sun was just peeking in the window. It was Christmas!

Jenny and Jeff got up from the chair and looked around the room. The big man with the funny beard was not there. They looked at each other curiously. "Was that...?" "Do you think...?" Neither of them finished their questions.

They looked at the creche table. The light was gone. The old Bible was back in place but something was different. They looked and looked and finally saw it: a new figure knelt in the creche scene! It was a man with a full white beard. His black boots and bright suit did not match the clothes on the other figures. The head was bowed and a thoughtful look was on the face with the smile lines. Anyone else looking at the new figure might have thought that it was there by mistake, that it should not have been a part of the scene with the wise men and shepherds and all. But Jeff and Jenny understood. They knew that the familiar figure really did belong right there where it was; kneeling at the manger.

Later that morning when Jeff and Jennifer opened their gifts, they were excited, of course, and happy with everything. But they couldn't forget how sad the large man in the red suit had looked when he said, "People sometimes forget that *my* gifts are supposed to remind them of the *greatest* Christmas gift of all, the Baby Jesus; God's gift to everyone.

Jenny and Jeff soon outgrew the toys and clothes they found under the tree that long-ago Christmas morning, but they never forgot that magic Christmas Eve when they learned the real meaning of the gifts of Christmas.

Questionnaire For Christmas

by Mabelle McGuire

Directions: Write the answers to the following questions. Keep them brief.

1. From what country do we get the hymn "Silent Night, Holy Night"?

2. From what country do we get the music for "O Come, All Ye Faithful"?

3. Where do we find children enjoying the "pinata"?

4. Where do children put out their shoes to receive gifts from St. Nicholas?

5. In what country do children hang up their stockings?

6. Who introduced Santa Claus and his "eight tiny reindeer"?

7. What is the name of the reindeer that joined the team almost a century later?

8. Where is it always warm on Christmas day except in the mountains?

9. To what town do thousands of pilgrims go to spend Christmas?

10. In what country is this town located?

Answers: 1 — Germany; 2 — Portugal; 3 — Mexico; 4 — Holland; 5 — USA; 6 — Dr. Clement Moore; 7 — Rudolph; 8 — any place on the equator; 9 — Bethlehem; 10 — Israel.

AN ADVENT CALENDAR GAME

by Jane Priewe

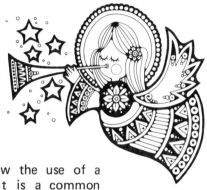

Every child comes to know the use of a calendar in their daily lives. It is a common commodity which keeps us ever aware of particular dates. We see Christmas drawing near, but without being reminded of the beautiful Christmas story.

An Advent calendar promises that a joyful, Christmas Day is on the way! It also is a daily challenge for children while they learn the tale of Christ's birth. This calendar starts with the first day of Advent and is an on-going puzzle-game until December 25th arrives.

If you decide to use this personal Advent calendar project, each child must have his/her own calendar sheet with blocks drawn on it for each day of the Advent season. For each calendar block, you must select a Bible passage relating to the Christmas story, plus a few Messianic promises as an introduction to the story.

Inside each block on the calendar print a few key words taken from a particular passage, beginning with the promises. For example, key words for Isaiah 7:14 could be *Virgin, Son, Immanuel* (Behold, a virgin shall conceive, and bear a son, and shall call his name Immanuel). Key words for Luke 2:4 could be *Joseph, Nazareth, David* (And Joseph went up from Galilee, out of the city of Nazareth, into Judea, unto the city of David, which is called Bethlehem; because he was of the house and lineage of David). Key words for Matthew 1:21 could be *bring forth, Jesus, people* (And she shall bring forth a son, and thou shalt call his name Jesus: for he shall save his people from their sins.)

Using adhesive backed paper, preferrably in bright colors, type the Bible passages which go with sets of key words already printed on calendar blocks. Cut the typed passages into squares so that the youngsters can stick them over the proper key word block on the calendar. Since each child will have his/her own set of Bible verse squares and a calendar to take home, finding the verse to stick over each day is to be a *daily* game. Stress that it is not fair to work ahead. At first, it will take longer to go through all the verses, but as days pass, and more key word sets are covered with a verse, the game will become easier.

To make this project as simple as possible for the teacher, blank calendar pages can be xeroxed, carbon copied or mimeographed. Matching verses which cover key words can also be carbon copied. The finished calendar is very colorful, and could be framed as a lasting remembrance of Christ's birth.

Preparing for this project does take time, but by starting on it well in advance of Advent, you will be ready with a key word calendar and an envelope of Bible verses for each child on the first Sunday of Advent. By searching through the verses every day to find the one which corresponds with a set of key words, children will unwittingly review the story of Christ's birth throughout the Advent season. They may find that they are actually memorizing some of the shorter Bible passages. But best of all, the true meaning and importance of the blessed holiday season unfolds for them.

Nov. 30	Dec. 1	Dec. 2	Dec. 3	Dec. 4	Dec. 5	Dec. 6
Behold a virgin shall conceive, and shall bear a Son, and shall call his name Immanuel	*When Israel was a child, then I loved him, and called my son out of Egypt*	Son	Mary	Decree	Joseph	Taxed
		Jesus	Soul	World	Nazareth	Wife
		People	Magnify	Taxed	David	Child
Is. 7:14	*Hosea 11:1*					
		(Matthew 1:21)	(Luke 1:46)	(Luke 2:1)	(Luke 2:4)	(Luke 2:5)

Sing A Song Of Christmas Carols

by Shirley P. Waite

It's that time of year! Every time you turn on the radio or television, you hear carols. And soon you find yourself humming them all day! So do the children you teach in church school. Christmas carols make you — and them — feel warm and happy inside. Then you all get enthused about the approaching holiday season.

Perhaps the children might wonder why Christmas songs are called carols. They may also enjoy knowing how the most popular carols came to be written. Why not share this information with them during Advent?

A long time ago, a carol wasn't singing at all. It was a group dance accompanied by a joyful song. But through the years, "carol" came to mean the song itself, and it is still joyful, because it tells about the glad news of Christ's birth.

Some carols are so old, nobody knows who wrote them. During the Middle Ages, much of the church music was chanted (a repetition of certain words in one tone.) The people in the churches wanted to liven up their music, so they began to dance to it.

THE FIRST NOEL

One of the first dance songs was **The First Noel** which was originally heard in England or France. Authorities cannot agree on what "Noel" means. Some say it comes from a Latin word "novella" which means "news." (Point out that this news is about the birth of a special baby.) Others think it is related to the word "natalis," which means "birthday", and still others think it might be a contraction for "Now all is well."

O COME ALL YE FAITHFUL

This is another carol which is so old nobody seems to know its story. The tune is similar to one from a French variety show; yet others say it is of British origin. In the 1800's it was even known as "The Portuguese Hymn." It was first sung in Latin, "Adeste Fidelis", before English words were written, and was a hymn of praise. One thing is certain — it is loved the world over.

A legend has sprung up that St. Francis of Assisi originated caroling. You may recall that this good saint set up the first Nativity scene near Grecchio, Italy. Quite likely, he sang the story of the first Christmas to the villagers. Later, as churches began to display Nativity scenes, the people participated; then the singing continued as they strolled through the villages. This is probably how our custom of carolling from door to door started.

JOY TO THE WORLD

What would you think of a man who was invited to spend a week visiting friends, and stayed thirty-six years? Isaac Watts did that very thing! During his long visit, he wrote many songs (we know of 454 in use today.) Like many of his other hymns, **Joy To The World** is based on a Psalm the 98th. (Look it up and see the similarities.) Isaac started writing poems when he was seven years old. He grew up believing that church singing should be happy, which was frowned upon in his day. Maybe his joyous outlook on life is why his hostess of thirty-six years declared that his visit was "the shortest" she had ever experienced!

HARK! THE HERALD ANGELS SING

There is one man who wrote far more hymns than Isaac Watts. His name was Charles Wesley, whose brother John was the founder of the Methodist Church. Charles wrote several thousand hymns! Surely with that many tunes to his credit, one must be a carol — and it was! You might not have recognized it at first — "Hark, how all the welkin rings, glory to the King of Kings." A friend of Wesley's, George Whitefield, persuaded him that the word "welkin" was awkward, and the song was changed to "Hark! the herald angels sing, Glory to the newborn King!" (You might suggest that the children look up the word "welkin". They will discover that it means "sky".) Charles wrote this beloved carol in 1739, but it was not until one hundred years later that Felix Mendelssohn wrote the music.

SILENT NIGHT

The most popular Christmas carol had its setting in an Austrian mountain village. The year was 1818. Father Joseph Mohr was very unhappy, because mice had nibbled at the bellows of the church organ. How could there be a Christmas Eve service with no music? The organist, Franz Gruber was unhappy too, because he didn't have the tools or training to fix the organ. The afternoon of December 24th, Father Mohr had been to a woodcutter's cottage to baptize a new baby. No doubt he thought about another birth on this same night, centuries before. Words came rushing to his mind. He hurried to ask Mr. Gruber if he could compose a simple tune. Christmas Eve the congregation was disappointed at first until, with Father Mohr singing and Franz Gruber strumming his guitar, they heard the beautiful words, "Silent Night, Holy Night." Mrs. Gruber said quietly to her husband, "We will die, you and I, but this song will live." And so it has!

AWAY IN A MANGER

Perhaps the first carol you sang as a small child was **Away in a Manger**. It's also known as "Luther's Cradle Hymn", although Martin Luther never heard it. Luther used to sing lullabies to his children as they went to sleep, a fact that prompted the unknown author of this carol to write, "Composed by Martin Luther for his children, and still sung by German mothers everywhere." Actually, **Away in a Manger** is an American carol. It may have first been sung among German people in Pennsylvania, which would account for the idea that it had German origin, as well as its widespread growth in America.

GOOD KING WENCESLAUS

Did you know that there really was a king by the name of Wenceslaus? He ruled Bohemia (Czechoslavakia) from 928 to 935 A.D. He was a very kind Christian ruler who helped the poor in his kingdom by taking them food and fuel. An Anglican minister, John Mason Meale wrote the words in the middle 1800's.

O LITTLE TOWN OF BETHLEHEM

About the same time that **Good King Wenceslaus** was written, an American minister took a trip to the Holy Land in 1865. He planned a horseback ride from Jerusalem to Bethlehem, so he could be there on the anniversary of Christ's birthday. As it began to get dark, he rode to the field where, tradition says, the shepherds were keeping their flocks by night. He visualized the scene — a quiet little town in the distance — the stars appearing, one brighter than the rest — it was breath-taking! Three years later, when Phillips Brooks was back in Philadelphia, preparing for Christmas, he decided to write a poem for the children of his church to recite. He asked Lewis Redner, the church organist, to compose music for his poem. Mr. Redner couldn't think of a tune, but the night before the Sunday School program, he woke up suddenly with a melody in his mind. So, over one hundred years ago, a group of children your own age sang **O Little Town of Bethlehem** for the first time.

We may get tired someday of listening to the popular songs we hear on the radio and delevision, but we never tire of Christmas carols, for they are eternal. They tell of the most important event in history — the birth of our Lord, Jesus, Christ!

Faith In God

by Elaine Ward

Story:

"It can't be! It's impossible!" The young girl could not understand!

Mary was like the other girls of her age. Her family was poor. She loved her brothers and sisters. She worked and prayed every day. Mary was like the other girls her age, except for one thing ... Mary had an amazing faith in God.

As Mary worked at her daily tasks, she often thought about God and about her people's hope. "Someday the Messiah will come. God's will will be done among us," Mary's father often said, as they lighted the oil in the small clay holder and gathered around the evening meal.

In the dim light Mary listened to his words. Sometimes her brothers paid no attention. Her sisters thought of other things, but Mary listened to her father's words and kept them in her heart.

Tonight she had heard new words. She had listened carefully to the angel, for they were strange words! How could she, a young, simple girl like all the other girls whom she knew, how could she become the mother of the Messiah?

The words were unbelievable and yet she kept them in her heart, for Mary was like the other girls her age except for one thing ... Mary had an amazing trust in God!

Soon it was time to go to Bethlehem. "We must go to be counted. I know that it is far and I wish there were some way that you could stay here until the baby is born, but Caesar has decreed that each one of us must be enrolled." Joseph looked into Mary's eyes. Her eyes always gave him hope. He wondered if it was because of her amazing trust in God.

It was hard for Mary to stay awake on the donkey. She was large and awkward with child. "Will we reach Bethlehem before the baby is born?" she asked herself over and over, as she rode the weary miles from Nazareth to Bethlehem.

"Mary! Mary! Wake up, there is Bethlehem ahead!" Joseph gently shook Mary awake.

"Yes, Joseph?" she said, trying to understand his words.

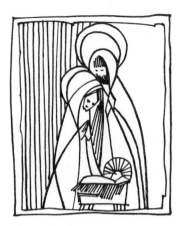

"Soon you will be safely asleep and warm with a pillow for your head. Mary, we are in Bethlehem."

Mary could scarcely believe Joseph's words. During the long, hard journey she often wondered if they would ever reach Bethlehem, if she would ever sleep under a roof again. She had a right to wonder, for Joseph's words were not so easily fulfilled.

Each time Joseph returned to Mary, his words were the same. "There is no room in Bethlehem. There is no place for us to stay!"

Mary smiled, as she touched Joseph's cheek, her eyes still full of hope, because of her amazing faith in God. "God will provide," she promised the man before her. He looked so tired and discouraged. "God's will will be done."

Joseph took courage and strength from Mary's words as he approached yet another inn.

"No, there is no room. What with the census, we have been filled for days," the man spoke hurridly, for he was busy and had little time to waste on a humble carpenter.

"But my wife is about to have a baby. We would be happy to share the stable with your animals, if only we could. She cannot go any further," Joseph pleaded.

The man glanced quickly at the woman on the donkey. Mary had again fallen asleep. He could see Joseph's words were true. "Then use the stable. I will send the boy out to sweep and make it clean."

"God bless you!" Joseph embraced the man.

It was late and dark in the stable when the baby was born that night in Bethlehem.

Mary listened to the words of the shepherds who had suddenly appeared from nowhere. They were strange words about angels' singing and a bright, golden star that hung over the stable. She did not understand all that they said. She was tired from the long journey and from the birth of the baby, but she kept the words in her heart.

"Someday, perhaps, I will understand," Mary thought, as she heard the jumbled words of the poor shepherds. "Now I must sleep so I can care for the baby. God will provide. God's will will be done among us."

The night was dark and cold and silent, as Mary slept. Mary, a girl like all other girls her age, except for her amazing faith in God, this Mary was now the mother of Jesus, the Messiah!

For Discussion:

What were the words that were hard for Mary to believe? Did she believe them? Why? Have you ever wondered why Mary was the mother of Jesus? What do you think? Does it matter if we have faith in God? How?

Prayer:

Dear God, give us an amazing faith that will help us have courage and hope and direction, in Christ's name. Amen.

To Do:

Make a Christmas paperweight. Thoroughly clean a round glass jar with a deep lid. Place a few teaspoons of plaster of paris in a cup. Mix with water until it is the consistency of thick pancake batter. Pour the plaster of paris mixture into the jar cover. Do not fill the lid; leave space at the top to screw onto the jar. Set a small plastic Christmas tree ornament in the plaster. Let it harden.

Fill the jar with clear water. Add finely ground moth flakes. Screw the cap with the attached ornament on tight. Turn it upside down. Shake it and you have a snowstorm.

CHILDREN'S CHIRSTMAS WORKSHOP

by Colleen Britton

The Christmas season is so filled with excitement, activities, and possibilities! What we always run short of is time. The short class time spent in church school each week didn't allow us the time necessary to provide the enrichment we wanted to give our children during Advent. We solved the problem with a Saturday Christmas Workshop. Our church had no social hall, so our home became the center of bustling holiday activity. A learning-activity center was placed in the kitchen, den, family room, living room, garage, patio, and even at the top of the stairs. It seemed that something exciting was happening in every nook and cranny.

The children gathered in the living room and after singing several Christmas carols and briefly explaining the activities at each center, we broke up into groups and began to explore the centers one by one. Simple directions were written out at each center and an older youth or adult was there to help. Soft Christmas music was played in the background and we all found ourselves humming and singing as we worked.

At the close of the workshop we gathered again to discuss what we had done, sing more songs, and of course, eat some Christmas cookies. Many of the decorations were shared with the rest of the congregation and a local convalescent home during Advent.

The possibilities for activity-learning centers are unlimited! Some of the activities that we have found most successful are listed below. Suggestions relating the activities to a total Advent program are also included.

GOLD FOIL ORNAMENTS (Symbols)

Materials needed: Patterns cut from poster board or other heavy paper, scissors, gold poster board, thread for hanging, hole punch or needle.

Trace patterns onto foil and cut out. Punch hole at top and attach thread for hanging.

Suggestions for use:
• Discuss the meaning and stories behind the various symbols
• Have children write the meaning of each symbol on back
• Several together create an interesting mobile for church school classroom, shut-in or home

FUN-STICK STAR (Hope)

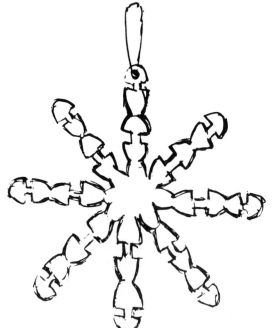

Materials needed: 4 funsticks per star (one with a small hole drilled at one end and a dot in the middle), (Note: funsticks are popsicle sticks with notches cut in them. They are avaiable at hobby and novelty stores) gold spray paint, glitter, nylon fishing line, white glue, newspaper or newsprint.

Place a small drop of glue on the dot in the center of the stick and add the other three sticks in an asterisk fashion. When the glue dries, place all stars on large sheets of newspaper or newsprint and spray with gold paint. While paint is still wet, sprinkle with glitter. Turn the star over and spray the other side. The paper underneath makes beautiful wrapping paper or bulletin board background. Tie fish line through hole for hanging.

Suggestions for use during Advent:
• Gifts for family, congregation, shut-ins, elderly
• Decorate a tree for the church, needy family, hospital
• Put several together for a mobile in shut-in's room

CANDY CANE MESSAGES (Joy)

Materials needed: 4-inch red pipe cleaners, 4-inch white pipe cleaners, green construction paper 2 x 3 inches approx., felt pen, safety pins or straight pins.

Hold one red and one white pipe cleaner together and twist. Form into a candy cane shape. Write "JOY" or some other Christmas message on paper and pin to candy cane.

Note: Even preschoolers can succeed at this project. Their messages can be written by an adult or could be a picture cut from a card.

Suggestions for use during Advent:
• Great gifts for the congregation on the Sunday before Christmas (Joy)
• Children from the church school classes can give these messages of "Joy" and "Hope" to patients at a convalescent home or hospital as part of a giving or caroling experience.

PINECONE CANDLE HOLDER

Materials needed: Small pinecones and nuts, 2½-inch styrofoam balls cut in half, 6-inch red candles, hot-melt glue, small heating plate and metal container (pie tin), brown spray paint.

Spray the styrofoam balls brown and cut in half. Place a red candle in the center. Dip small pine cones and nuts into hot melt glue and press into the styrofoam.

Suggestions for use:
• Gifts for parents, teachers, pastor
• Children could present them at homes of elderly while caroling
• Candle light can be related to Christ, the light of the world
• Cones and nuts can be related to the potential of new life found in Christ

DOVE ORNAMENT/MOBILE (Peace, Holy Spirit)

Materials needed: Thin sheets of styrofoam, meat trays or poster board, poster board patterns, scissors, fishing line, transparent tape.

Trace pattern onto styrofoam or posterboard and cut out. Insert wings into slot in body and secure with transparent tape. Hang with fish line.

Suggestions for use:
• Tree ornament for church tree, family tree
• Several can be hung from a small dowell and used as a mobile for a shut-in's room
• Give them as gifts when your group goes caroling
• Can also be used with a lesson about Baptism

COMMUNION CUP BELL (Joy, Communion)

Materials needed: Plastic communion cups, small metal bells, wire, white glue, glitter, soldering iron or something to melt hole in bottom of cup.

The joy of Christmas, the joy of Christ's coming can be related to the joy of communion by making communion bell ornaments. Holes are made in the bottom of clear plastic communion cups with the small tip of a hot soldering iron. The rim of the cups are dipped in white glue and then into glitter. When they are dry, small metal bells are strung inside with a wire which also serves as a hanger.

Suggestions for use:
• Ornaments can be given to the congregation as part of a Communion service during Advent.
• Can be used as tray favors in hospitals

CHRISTMAS STORY CENTER

Materials needed: A wide selection of Christmas stories, books and magazines which children can look through and read to one another.

TIN CAN LANTERNS (Light of the World)

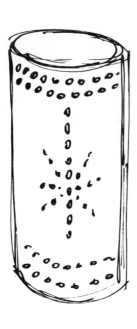

Materials needed: Soup cans filled with frozen water, hammer, large nails, paper to fit around cans (wrong side of labels work well), tape, pencil, gloss black spray paint, votive candle.

Draw simple designs on paper — crosses, asterisk stars, etc. Tape paper to can and pound nails along the lines. The more holes you have, the more light will come through. When design is completed, remove ice and spray with gloss black paint. Place votive candle inside.

Suggestions for use:
• Relate to lesson about Christ, the Light of the World
• Use to light sanctuary for Christmas Eve service.
• Use in window to let the Light of Christ shine in your home during Advent

BREAD DOUGH ORNAMENTS

Materials needed: 2 cups flour, 1 cup salt, 1 cup or less of water (add gradually), food coloring, cookie sheet, oven.

Shape dough into a ball and kneed 5-10 minutes until smooth. Add food coloring if desired. Make ornaments, insert paperclip into top for hanging. Place on cookie sheet and bake at 325 degrees until hard. Ornaments can be painted with a gloss finish if desired.

Suggestions for use:
• Make ornaments into shapes of Christian symbols: cross, dove, butterfly; characters from the Christmas story; spell words like Joy, Hope, Love, Peace, children's names
• Use ornaments to decorate a Chrismon tree (a tree decorated with symbols of Christ)
• Larger ornaments can be hung in children's rooms

SARDINE CAN ORNAMENTS

Materials needed: Sardine cans with small hole punched in top center, assorted Christmas cards and trims, scissors, glue, 4-inch pipe cleaners.

Sardine cans can become exquisite little Christmas shadow boxes. This is an activity which can be enjoyed by children of all ages. Portions of Christmas cards are cut out and glued onto the can — front edge, back, wherever desired. Trims and glitter may also be desired. You may want to suggest that students try to show one of the themes of Advent: Love, Hope, Peace, Joy, or the Christmas story. Insert a looped pipe cleaner through the hole in the top for hanging.

Suggestions for use:
- Gifts for family, shut-ins
- Decorations for church tree

ICED CHRISTMAS COOKIES

Materials needed: Un-iced cookies, icing of various colors, sugar sprinkles, several spreading knives, cookie sheets or several large plates.

This is a good center to locate near the kitchen sink, as children can be messy! Let them put icing on the cookies and decorate as they desire.

Suggestions for use:
- Cookies can be shared with the congregation during the fellowship time after services.
- Plates of several cookies can be wrapped up and taken to shut-ins as a gift from the children.
- Broken cookies can be eaten by the children at the close of the workshop

CLOTHES PIN ANGEL

Materials needed: Pattern, push clothes pin, 2 paper baking cups, yarn, scissors, glue, colored paper, wrapping paper, glitter, assorted trims, fine line felt pens.

Trace dress pattern onto colored paper and cut out. Draw face on angel head with the split side of the clothes pin facing up. Flatten baking cups, cut about a quarter out of the circle for wings. Glue dress to front of clothes pin and wings to the back. Note: Glue only down to the split of the clothes pin so the pin will fit over the branch without tearing the dress or wings. Glue several 1-inch pieces of yarn to the head for hair. Add trims to dress if desired and glitter to wings.

Suggestions for use:
- Relate to angels spreading the Joy of Christ's birth
- Tree ornament for church or home

FELT STAINED GLASS

Materials needed: Scraps of colored felt, black felt for background, scissors, white glue.

Scraps of colored felt can become a beautiful stained glass banner. Use a background of black felt. Choose a simple subject such as the cross, a candle, bells, etc. Glue on scraps of colored felt to depict the central subject, then fill in the background. Remember to leave space between the pieces so that the black shows through.

Suggestions for use:
• Decorations for classroom, sanctuary, family home, patients' doors, etc.
• Black can be applied to a larger colored background to make a larger banner. Several can be grouped together.
• It can be glued to a toilet paper roll, hung with a pipe cleaner to make a hanging ornament

YARN ORNAMENTS (Christian symbols)

Materials needed: Symbol patterns, meat trays or cardboard, yarn, liquid starch, scissors, pins, wax paper, glitter, fishing line, damp cloth for sticky fingers.

Cut lengths of yarn long enough to trace design. Dip yarn in dish of starch and let stand for several minutes so that the yarn absorbs the glue. Place patterns on top of styrofoam trays or cardboard. Place wax paper over patterns. Pull yarn from starch removing excess. Begin by placing one end of the yarn at a corner and hold it in place with pins wherever necessary. Trim excess yarn. Sprinkle glitter on the wet yarn and let dry (overnight). Separate yarn from wax paper or cut around edges and leave wax paper attached. Use fishing line for hanging.

Suggestions for use:
• Decorations for a church or family tree
• With wax paper left on, yarn symbols can be used as the cover of Christmas cards to be sent to children in other parts of the world, shut-ins, etc.

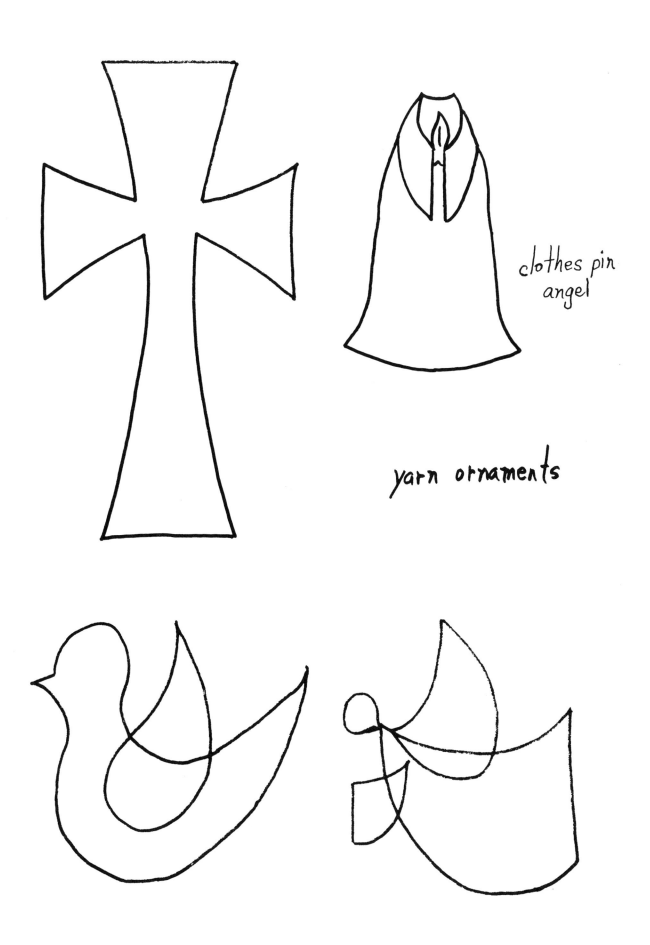

clothes pin
angel

yarn ornaments

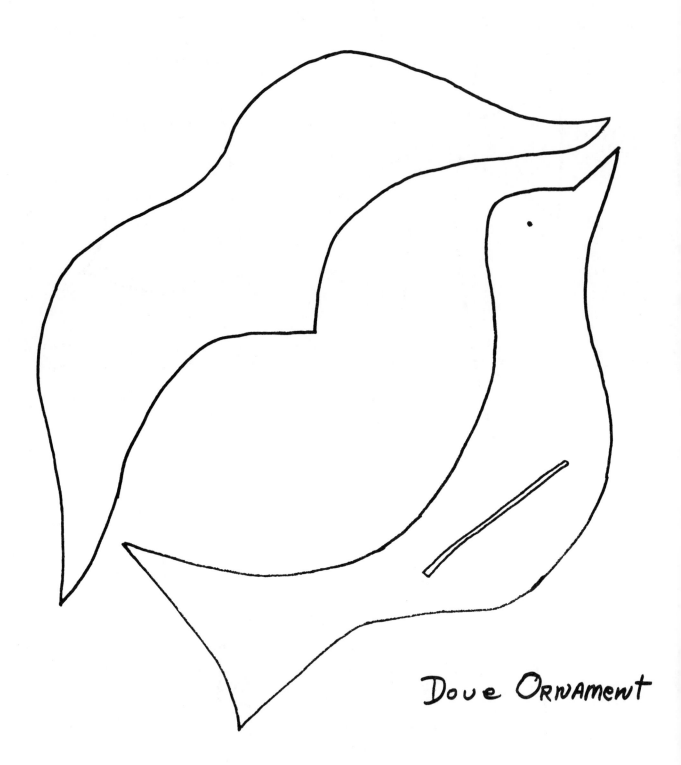

Dove Ornament

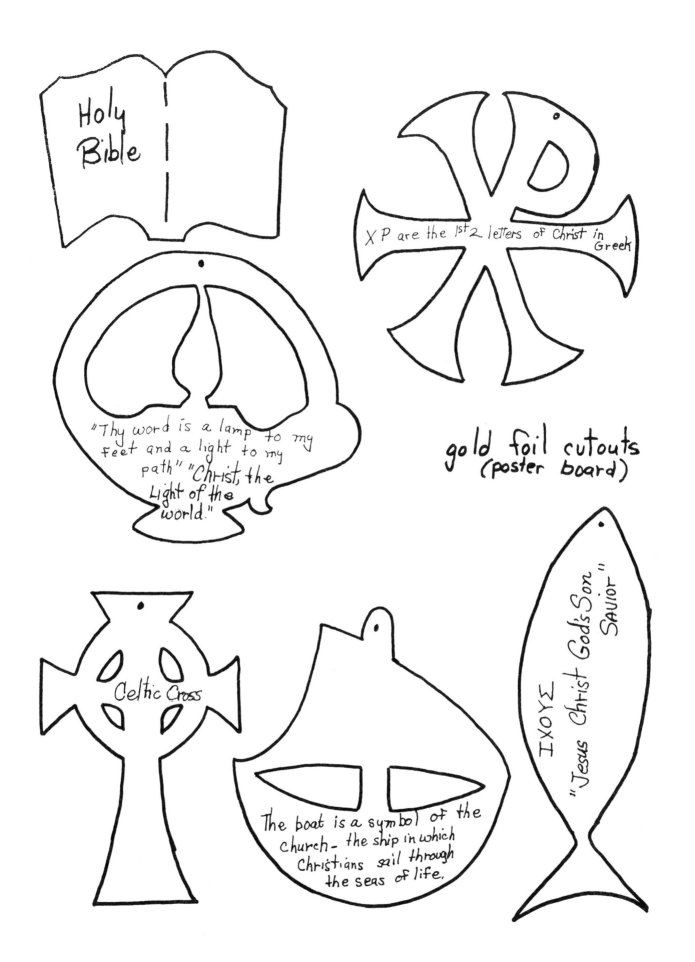

Holy Bible

XP are the 1st 2 letters of Christ in Greek

"Thy word is a lamp to my feet and a light to my path" "Christ, the Light of the world."

gold foil cutouts
(poster board)

Celtic Cross

The boat is a symbol of the church— the ship in which Christians sail through the seas of life.

IXOYΣ
"Jesus Christ God's Son" Savior

—59—

CHRISTMAS TREE

by Mabelle McGuire

Directions: Draw a line around each of the words that are printed backward, forward, up, down, and diagonally. Check the list. The isolated letters that read from left to right spell a hidden word.

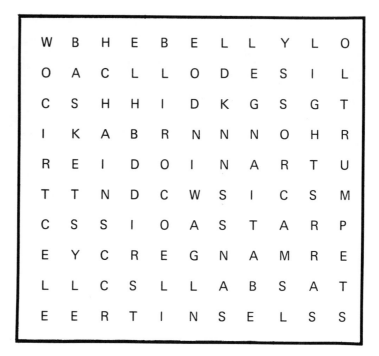

W	B	H	E	B	E	L	L	Y	L	O
O	A	C	L	L	O	D	E	S	I	L
C	S	H	H	I	D	K	G	S	G	T
I	K	A	B	R	N	N	N	O	H	R
R	E	I	D	O	I	N	A	R	T	U
T	T	N	D	C	W	S	I	C	S	M
C	S	S	I	O	A	S	T	A	R	P
E	Y	C	R	E	G	N	A	M	R	E
L	L	C	S	L	L	A	B	S	A	T
E	E	R	T	I	N	S	E	L	S	S

ANGEL, BALL, BASKET, BELLS, BOWS, CANDLE, CHAINS, CHRISTMAS, COW, CROSS, DOLL, DONKEY, ELECTRIC, ICICLE, LIGHTS, MANGER, STAR, TINSELS, TRAIN, TREE, TRUMPETS.

Answer: The hidden word is HOLIDAYS.

WORKING ADVENT CALENDAR

by Colleen Britton

The lighting of Advent candles has been a tradition in our congregation for many years. Each Sunday of Advent the children anxiously await that part of the worship service when they can light the candles and respond to questions about the meaning of each — Hope, Love, Peace, Joy and the Christ candle.

Last year we decided to further emphasize the meaning of the Advent season by having the children in the church school make "working Advent wreath calendars". Twenty four simple tasks aimed at helping the child further prepare for Christmas, the celebration of Christ's birth, were typed and individually pasted onto folded pieces of contruction paper cut into the shapes of holly

berries, leaves, candles, and flames. Each shape was numbered, taped closed, and then glued onto a 12 x 18 inch piece of blue construction paper by the children.

Each day of Advent the children opened one of the shapes and did whatever task was written there. We found that the calendar helped the youth grasp the idea of Advent as a time of preparation. It also suggested activities which included the family and congregation together in these Advent preparations.

Below is the list of suggestions that we used. I am sure you will want to add some of your own.
1. Make up a thank you prayer.
2. Write a letter to a grandparent.
3. Help with the dishes.
4. Help someone with their job.
5. Make and send a Christmas card.
6. Pray the Lord's prayer.
7. Do something for Mom and Dad.
8. Help set the table.
9. Do something nice for a teacher.
10. Make a Christmas ornament.
11. Share something with a friend.
12. Find the Christmas story in the Bible (Luke 2).
13. Make up a Christmas poem.
14. Clean up your room.
15. Make a gift for someone.
16. Sing a Christmas carol.
17. Pray for someone you love.
18. Make a Christmas picture for your home.
19. Find the Chrismtas story in Matthew 2.
20. Bake some Christmas cookies.
21. Keep a promise.
22. Pray for a joyful Christmas.
23. Visit a friend.
24. Give a gift to someone.

List of suggestions is from PREPARING FOR THE MESSIAH by Doris Williams and Patricia Griggs.

Ceremony of the Gifts

by Jill R. Edens

Ask any child what he or she thinks of when you say "Christmas," and you are likely to get "presents!" as your answer. While we may be disappointed that the Nativity story isn't the first thing children think of, we might do well to capitalize on their natural inclination toward gift giving. This is the purpose of the following children's worship idea — to help children expand their view of what gift giving is really all about.

Begin by having the class wrap empty boxes to look like Christmas gifts. Children will enjoy working with wrapping paper, ribbon, and brightly colored stickers. When each child has wrapped a box, pass out white tags. Ask the children if they can think of words that represent spiritual gifts and record them on the chalkboard as the children think of them. Words like "love", "peace", "friendship", "hope", are all appropriate responses. When all have chosen their words, they may write them on their white tags and fasten them to their packages.

Worship time may then begin. The class should be invited to gather around a brightly lighted Christmas tree in a darkened room where they may begin worship with some familiar Christmas carols followed by a short prayer. The worship leader might then instruct the young people to think of those in the room to whom they would like to give their spiritual gifts. When each child has thought of someone and has mentally given the spiritual gift represented on the package, the children may quietly move forward and place their packages under the Christmas tree before returning to their places. (Background music is helpful during this part of the service.) When every package is under the tree, the service may be ended with the singing of another carol, followed by a friendship circle around the tree.

Christmas Reminder Hunt

by Verna Schmidt

Does your church customarily provide bags of candy to children at Christmas time? If so, make it a fun and learning experience by creating a "Christmas Reminder Hunt" by attaching a sheet to the bag of selected candy. (Hint: Purchase bags of miniature packs of Life Savers at Halloween time, since only large packs are sold at Christmas time.)

Example of sheet:

Match treats in this bag with reminders of Christmas. Use names or the way they look as clues.

1. A little _____ was born in Bethlehem.
2. An _____ told shepherds good news.
3. Shepherds use _____ to catch lambs.
4. A _____ shone in the sky.
5. One of the Wise Men gave a gift of _____.
6. Another gift was probably brought inside of a _____.
7. Hear the _____ ring out the good news.
8. Jesus, our Savior, is our _____ _____.
9. Since we need not worry with Jesus at our side, our lives are _____.

Answers:

1. baby (licorice or chocolate babies)
2. angel (foil-wrapped angel figures)
3. crooks (peppermint candy canes)
4. star (white chocolate star or Starburst cube)
5. gold (one of the gold-foil wrapped coin shapes found in "bags of gold" chocolate)
6. barrel (root beer barrel)
7. bell (chocolate or cream-filled bells found wherever Christmas candy is)
8. Life Saver
9. Carefree (stick of Carefree gum)

OUR CHRISTMAS PROJECT

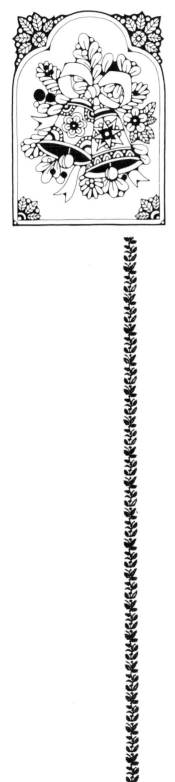

by Thelma Collums

Soon the children, though small in number due to a rainy night and due to illness, were back at the church telling everyone they met about their fun project. The group had learned much by doing and enjoyed every minute of it while sharing with others.

"How many would like to do something real nice this Christmas for some sweet older ladies?" Mrs. Hall asked her class.

"They are as old or older than your grandmothers," she said.

Hands began to rise from one side of the group to the other until all hands except John's were raised.

"John, don't you want to do something nice to help some ladies?" asked Tamara as she tapped him on his knee.

John was busy looking at the stick puppet of Paul, which he had made during activity time.

"Yes, I was going to raise my hand," he replied, and up it went.

"A nursing home is only a few blocks away. There are many people who are not as fortunate as we are. For some, just walking is very hard. They move in wheelchairs, but most of them can go to their meals, enjoy birthday parties and games in the dining room. They like seeing the T. V. programs in the living room, too. It is fun for friends to go with them for an outside walk, or take them for a ride when the weather is nice like today. But everyone is not able to do these exercises. Some cannot leave their beds and must be helped. It would be good if we could do something for all. I want you to suggest what we might do for our project this Christmas.

"Mrs. Hall," Marissa asked, "could we go to see them?"

"I wish we could take them something," said David.

"Both of your suggestions are fine," Mrs. Hall said with a smile as the others expressed their wishes.

"Forty-eight ladies are living in the home and we have eleven children in this group. Some do not attend regularly, so whatever we carry will have to cost very little," Mrs. Hall explained.

"Everyone think hard for a minute of something we might take each lady," suggested Mrs. Hall.

Toothbrushes, soap, bath cloths, fruit, candy and a Christmas tree were among the suggestions. The group decided bath cloths would be nice for everyone and to get a small tree on which they could be tied would be just right. The group could meet early and decorate the tree with forty-eight bath cloths tightly wrapped in foil paper of different colors.

The tree was a three-foot cedar brought from the country by Mrs. Hall. It was cut with a small amount of the roots remaining. This was wrapped with cloth, pushed into a half-gallon fruit juice can and filled with gravel for balancing. A sheet of red construction paper was taped around the can. To that a brightly colored Christmas card, bearing names of all children, was taped on it with scripture verses dotted here and there as the children wished.

Not only did the group look with pleasure at the small tree topped by a foil-covered star which they provided, but eyes of the patients sparkled as they smiled and commented with happy remarks. The tree was placed on a side table to be enjoyed a few days before the gifts were given. Chairs, sofas, and wheelchairs were lining the walls of the living room and seated were many ladies smiling their sweetest smiles. They were beautiful with some wearing Sunday dresses on which were Christmas corsages, while others were dressed in pretty robes. Heads of white or graying hair with becoming makeup under the soft lights made a pretty picture. All seemed to be awaiting the 6:15 p.m. visit of the six and seven-year-old group from the church.

Brief practice periods two Sunday evenings before had each child knowing the first thing he was to do after arriving at the home. He was to listen quietly as each lady told her name. Next, each child was to tell his/her name. Three scripture verses relating to Christmas, including John 3:16, were quoted in unison with a certain child leading the group. Following the scripture two songs were sung. They were "Away in a Manger" (Murray) and "Silent Night" (Mohr.) The child leading the second song asked the ladies to help sing a verse of that song. They sang with smiles on their happy faces.

The program was over. "Good-byes" were heard as wishes for a Merry Christmas and hand waving went on until the last child passed through the door.

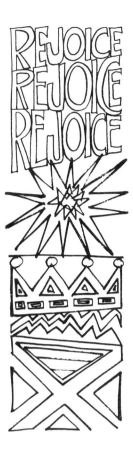

Activities For Advent

by Elaine Ward

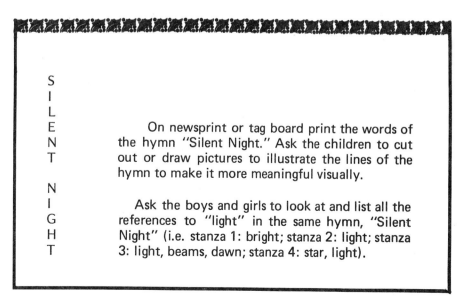

CHORAL READING

Read aloud Isaiah 9:6, inviting the group to prepare a choral reading. Write the words on newsprint or the blackboard for all to read. Talk about their meaning. Read the words together to feel their mood and rhythm. Divide the verse, such as:

Girls: **For to us a child is born,**
Boys: **To us a son is given;**
Girls: **And the government will be upon his shoulder,**
Boys: **And his name will be called** (Assign one individual for each of the following titles of the Messiah or ask the entire group to say them together:) **Wonderful Counselor, Mighty God, Everlasting Father, Prince of Peace.**

Tape the speaking. Listen with the group to appreciate the strong spots and correct any weak spots. They may wish to choose a recording, such as Christmas music without singing, as background music for their final taping. Use the tape in a worship service.

SILENT NIGHT

On newsprint or tag board print the words of the hymn "Silent Night." Ask the children to cut out or draw pictures to illustrate the lines of the hymn to make it more meaningful visually.

Ask the boys and girls to look at and list all the references to "light" in the same hymn, "Silent Night" (i.e. stanza 1: bright; stanza 2: light; stanza 3: light, beams, dawn; stanza 4: star, light).

Use the following poem, "The Colors of Christmas,"[1] giving each child a sheet of red, white, blue, gray, brown, purple, and gold (yellow) construction paper or dividing the colors among the children to be held above the head when they are mentioned.

Each color has a feeling,
Each color has a smell.
At Christmastime the colors have
A story that they tell.
Red
The red sunset reminded him of home.
How far they had come!
The sand was drenched in red, the rocks, the stones.
They talked together in quiet tones,
Walking their way to Bethlehem,
As Joseph prayed aloud, "God be with us all. Amen."
Blue
The wing of a bird,
The sea, the sky,
Blue is the mother Mary's cry
In reply to the cold and careless town,
Blue is the color of her gown.
Gray
Hungry and weary
From walking all day,
I covered the donkey
In soft shades of gray.
White
White the moonlight,
White the dove,
While the angels sing above,
Pure and white,
That Christmas night,
Telling shepherds of God's love.
Brown
Brown, brown the shepherds' coats,
Brown their lambs and brown their goats,
Brown the stable, brown the hay,
Brown the manger where he lay,
Sand and dust and trees and ground,
God must like the color brown.
Purple
From painting sunsets
To robing kings,
Purpleing pansies
And flamingo wings,
Mountains and shadows,
Midnight's trees,
Purple's purpose is to please.
Gold
Gold is a color, the coin of a king.
Some people think gold can buy anything . . .
Fame and friendship, forgiveness, joy,
A faraway castle, a magic toy,
Love and wisdom, travel abroad,
Once wisemen used it to praise their God!

CONVERSATION

Turn off the lights and darken the room. Talk about how the participants feel in the dark and what they think about the dark. "Suppose you felt as if you were in the dark all the time. What would you do? What would you want?"

The people of God felt they were in "the dark", that is, that they needed "light," God's light, a Savior. The prophet Isaiah wrote about the Hebrews' hope for light. We read his words during Advent. *"The people who walked in darkness have seen a great light; those who dwelt in a land of deep darkness, on them has light shined."* Isaiah 9:2

Turn on the light. Ask, "How do you feel about the light as it is turned on?" Listen to their responses and speak only after they have expressed their thoughts and feelings. "At first the light hurts our eyes. We are unaccustomed to it, much as the light from the heaven hurt the shepherds' eyes, when Jesus was born. At first, as the shepherds, we are numb with surprise. Then suddenly we appreciate the light and run to find its source and understand its meaning. We learn hymns, hear stories from the Bible, and study the scriptures in order to understand the source and meaning of the light.

BANNERS

Make Advent Banners. Small banners can be made from paper or felt individually or in groups of twos and threes. Have available explanations of the following symbols:

Advent wreath is round, green, no beginning, no ending as a symbol of eternity, and God's love everlasting.

Christmas tree is green, evergreen as a symbol of life.

Dove is a symbol of peace and of Jesus' baptism and the Holy Spirit.

Bell is a symbol for the call to worship.

Crown represents the three kings and their gifts for the Christ child.

Wrapped present is the symbol for God's love in giving His only Son.

Bible is a symbol of the story of God's love.

Shepherd's cane represents the shepherds who came to worship.

Musical note represents the angels' song of joy and good news.

Cross is a sign for the birth of the savior of the world.

Star could represent "light", as it led both the shepherds and the wise men in finding the Christ.

P
O
E
M

Use creche figures to tell the Christmas story in the following poem, "A Christmas Scene."[2]

Here's a stable safe and strong,
Here's a mother with her song,
Here's a father with his care,
Here's a shepherd with his prayer.
Here's a manger, here's a star,
Here's a wise man from afar,
Here's a Baby, here's a dove,
Here's a picture of God's love.

W
R
E
A
T
H
S

Make Advent wreaths, using five candles. The Christian Church uses the candle as its symbol of "light". It reminds us of him who is the "light of the world", as Jesus said in John 8:12: *"I am the light of the world. Whoever follows me will have the light of life and will never walk in darkness."*

The four candles of the Advent wreath could represent peace, hope, love and joy, surrounding the fifth candle, which is white for purity and the Messiah's birth. Each Sunday one candle is lit until Christmas, when the last, the fifth candle is lighted. The four candles may be purple or red.

A
V
I
S
I
T

Visit the sanctuary to see the Christmas tree or Advent wreath. Explain their meanings and ask one or more of the children to lead the class in prayer. Invite a musician (parent or choir member) to play Christmas music and carols the children can sing.

[1]Ward, Elaine M. **New Testament Stories**, Educational Ministries, Inc., Brea, CA, 1984.

[2]Ward, Elaine M. **Be and Say a Fingerplay**, Educational Ministries, Inc., Brea, CA, 1981.

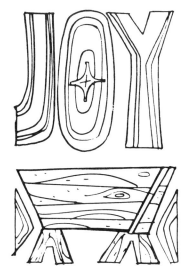

CELEBRATING

by Robert G. Davidson

Children live in the spirit of celebration discovery, joy and becoming. Children feel the excitement of anticipation but also live completely in the here and the now. Somewhere along the path to adulthood many persons lose their ability to celebrate the ordinary events and happenings of life. Why it happens, we are not sure. Could it be because we have been told that it is childish to take time to celebrate a new day, the beauty of a first rose, the freshness of a summer rain, or the first snow of winter?

Adults should make the most of the openness and spontaneity which children have in the ability to celebrate those temporary and special moments in life. We should expand their world and associate God with the happy and meaningful events in their lives. It can be our hope that children will grow up seeing religious faith as a joyful celebration of life.

BEGINNING CONVERSATION — Show the children several pictures which depict people celebrating different events in life. Include one picture of a worship service taking place. One picture might show a person holding a flower and another might portray two children talking or sharing something. Invite the children to share their thoughts and feelings about each picture as you hold them up one at a time. Give children in the group an opportunity to share their thoughts with the class if they wish.

The following questions might be helpful in leading the conversation:

• What do you see happening in this picture?

• What do you think they are celebrating in this picture?

• What kind of special things do you celebrate?

• How do you feel when you are celebrating something special?

• What makes something special enough to celebrate it as a special event?

SECOND CONVERSATION — Show the picture of the worshipping congregation again to the group. Spend a few minutes sharing with the children these thoughts and letting them respond. "Celebration is a time when we are happy. It is a special time — sometimes it is just for a moment. We celebrate life because of special events and happenings. We also believe life to be a special gift that God has given to each of us. Worship is a special time when we gather with our friends to celebrate and praise God."

THIRD CONVERSATION — Read the children the birth story from the Bible. Discuss why Jesus' birth is special and why we celebrate it. Talk about birthdays and parties. Suggest that they sing "Happy Birthday" to Jesus on Christmas day at home. Most of them have probably seen "The Little Drummer Boy" on television. Ask what gift they would give to the baby Jesus. Does giving a gift help make a celebration special?

A RAMBLE-SCRAMBLE

by Mabelle McGuire

Directions: Unscramble the words and write the correct spelling after each one.

1. Schirmats

2. Hemblehet

3. Murajeles

4. Elageli

5. Edjua

6. Dehro

7. glenas

8. vainitty

9. lestab

10. dherphess

Answers:
1. Christmas
2. Bethlehem
3. Jerusalem
4. Galilee
5. Judea
6. Herod
7. angels
8. nativity
9. stable
10. shepherds

Find Your Friend

by Mabelle McGuire

To find the name of the one whose birthday we celebrate in Advent, cross out the letter that is repeated the most in the diagram.

```
J   O   E   O
S   U   O   S
C   O   H   R
I   S   O   T
```

Answer: Jesus Christ

Helping By Not Helping

by N. Raymond Day

There are times when the best way to help others is not to help them at all.

The following is intended only as a guide. The person leading the children is encouraged to adapt it to his/her own style. A small blanket is needed as an aid.

Dialogue:

1. Ask: "Who can tell me where Mary and Joseph stayed when they came to Bethlehem that first Christmas a long time ago?" *(Permit replies)*

2. When appropriate say: "That's right. They stayed in a cave where animals were kept."

3. Ask: "Did they have lots of help finding a place to stay?" *(Permit replies)*

4. Continue: "They did not have very much help at all; and, I'll bet they were frightened, just like we get frightened when we are traveling and look for a motel room and find all the motels are full. How many of you have ever had that happen? Raise your hands if you have."

5. Continue: "It can be very frightening not to find help when you need it. But, you know what, it can also be frightening (or frustrating or angering) to *get* help sometimes. Do you believe that is possible? How many believe it can be troubling to have someone help you sometimes? Raise your hands if you think so."   ➔

6. Say: "Let's see if we can understand how helping someone can be frightening or upsetting to that person sometimes. I have a question for you. How many of you have been helping Mom and Dad get ready for Christmas? Raise your hands if you have." Tell me what you have been doing to be helpful."

7. Continue: "It's fun to help with all those things. But, you know, I'll bet Mom or Dad, at least once, has said something like this to you (make the following statement slowly and distinctly): 'I don't need your help right now; I'd rather do what I am doing all by myself.' Raise your hand if you have ever heard that from one of your folks."

8. Continue: "Let's see if we can understand why Mom or Dad might say that to us, by thinking what we can do with this blanket that I brought with me. What can we do with this blanket to help someone?"

9. Take the blanket and put it around the shoulders of a child close to you as you say: "We can help John (or whoever) keep warm by putting this blanket over his shoulders, and that would be helpful. But, what if I put the blanket over his head like this (place blanket over the child's head and hold it firmly against his face for a moment)? What would happen?" (Remove blanket and permit replies. Also ask the child over whose head and shoulders you placed the blanket: "When did you feel I was NOT helping you? Did you want THAT HELP when I gave it to you?")

10. "You see, sometimes we can actually frighten or hurt someone, or make them angry, by trying to help them. Each of us has to try to see when it is best to help someone by not helping that person. The next time Mom or Dad says, 'I don't need your help right now,' you say,'O.K., I'll go read, or color, or play with a friend.' If you do, I am certain that will make Mom or Dad very happy."

An Advent Session For Children

by Elaine Ward

Make Advent Wreaths. Have prepared play dough or materials for the children to mix and make the wreaths. You will need: a bowl, spoon, 1 cup salt, 2 cups flour, ½ tablespoon salad oil, and water to mix into a workable consistency. Add spice and red or green food coloring if desired for fragrance and decoration. Paper plates, 4 red or purple and 1 white candle for each child and glitter are also needed. Form dough into wreath shape on a paper plate. Add candles and glitter.

Say together an Advent fingerplay.

OUR ADVENT WREATH[1]

Here is our wreath, it's round and green.
Inside five candles can be seen. (hold up five fingers)
The first we light (hold up thumb) four weeks before
The birth of Him whom we adore.
The next Sunday we light one more. (hold up first finger)
Next week the third, (second finger) and sing and pray,
Soon we are lighting (third finger) candle four.
And then on Christmas Day just one more (fourth finger)
While someone reads the Christmas story (palms up as book)
That tells of Jesus' birth and of God's glory!

Light the Advent Wreath saying: "We have come together to think about Advent and Jesus' birth. We light this candle and thank you, dear God, for loving us. Let us pray, 'Dear God, as we get ready for the birthday of your son, Jesus Christ, we thank you for all of your gifts of love to us. We know that you are with us and love us always. Amen.' "

Hold Bible and Read: *"The people who walked in darkness have seen a great light; ...For to us a child is born, to us a son is given."* (Isaiah 9:2a, 6a)

Tell the Story, "The Fir":

Advent is getting ready for Jesus' birth. It is said, because Christmas is full of love and surprise, that on Christmas Eve all living creatures journey to Bethlehem to honor the newborn king and give him gifts.

There were murmurs in the woods. "Have you heard?" "Did you know?" "A king is born?" "Let us go!"

The trees of the forest were very excited. "All living creatures are going to Bethlehem to honor the newborn king and give him presents," they told one another.

Each of them began to plan what they would bring. "I will give him tasty, ripe olives," said the olive tree.

"I will share my delicious dates," planned the palm.

"I will take him the biggest, juiciest piece of fruit I have," promised the apple, the pear, and the peach trees.

The small fir tree was sad. It had no fruit to bring, no olives nor dates, nor apples, pears, or peaches. "What does one give a king?" the small fir tree wondered.

While the others were picking and planning, the little fir tree thought and thought. "What can I give the Baby?"

"Of course, he will bless me for such tasty olives," said the olive tree.

"Yes, of course," agreed the palm, doubtfully, "but my dates are delicious, and I do believe he will prefer my gift."

"Perhaps," interrupted the apple tree. "There is, however, nothing better than a ripe, red apple."

"Unless it is an orange!" cried the orange tree.

"Because the Baby has no teeth, I will bring him my softest peach," whispered the peach tree.

"And I my pear. We will see whose gift is best," added the proud pear tree.

The small fir tree said nothing, for it had nothing to say, but even worse, it had nothing to give. "What does one give a king?" worried the small tree.

When the trees had gathered their gifts, they happily marched through the woods with the other living creatures on their way to Bethlehem. There was the dog and the fox, the owl and the ox, the cock and the crow, the rat and the cat, the deer and the doe, all living creatures both large and small. There were the trees, the apple and the palm, the cherry and the olive, the peach and the pear, the ash and the aspen, and at the very end of the long procession came the small fir tree.

"Hurry up, Fir," called the aspen to the little fir at the end of the line.

"Oh, leave him alone. He doesn't even have a gift," growled the old elm.

The needles of the small fir tree drooped sadly from the branches hanging at its sides. "What does one give a king?" worried the little fir tree, trudging on.

At last they reached the stable in Bethlehem, but the little fir was too small to see the stall. "It doesn't matter. I do not deserve to see the Baby. I have no gift."

The little fir thought and thought. "A king deserves the very best. What is the best thing of all?" Suddenly the needles on its branches straightened, for the little tree now knew ...the best thing of all is love! "The best is love. I will give the king my love!"

No sooner had the fir tree said these words than the shining stars floating in the sky came closer and closer until they rested lightly on the fir tree's branches, as candles shining in the night. The Baby saw the light and it was a lovely sight, and the Baby smiled.

From that night the fir tree has been filled with bright, shining lights, reminding us that the best gift of all is love, God's love to all of us.

Sing a Christmas Carol.

[1]Ward, Elaine M. **Be and Say a Fingerplay**, Educational Ministries, Inc., Brea, CA, 1981.

Have You Seen the Baby Jesus?

Jill R. Edens

This Epiphany dramatization is designed to involve children in reviewing what they have learned about Christmas.

Setting: Sunday morning sanctuary service.

Minister: I would like to invite the church school young people to join me here in the chancel. (When the children settle into their places, three adults dressed as the Wise Men enter from the back of the sanctuary and proceed down the aisle toward the children.)

1st Wise Man: Has anyone seen the baby Jesus?

2nd Wise Man: We have seen his star in the East.

3rd Wise Man: Can you tell us where we can find him?

Minister: Wait a minute! Who are you anyway?

1st Wise Man: I am Jasper.

2nd Wise Man: I'm Balthasar.

3rd Wise Man: I'm Melchoir.

Wise Men: We are the Wise Men from the East and we seek the baby Jesus. Can you tell us where to find him?

Minister: I'm not sure that I can answer all of your questions — maybe the children can help. (Allow enough time for the children to respond to each question.)

1st Wise Man: Tell us, what is his mother's name?

2nd Wise Man: Yes, and what is his father's name?

3rd Wise Man: In what city was he born?

1st Wise Man: Why did his parents travel to Bethlehem?

2nd Wise Man: Where might we find him in Bethlehem?

3rd Wise Man: Thank you, boys and girls. This has been most helpful, but now we must be moving on to Bethlehem, for we have been traveling a long time and we are anxious to see the baby Jesus.

(Wise men exit. Children return to their seats.)

This dramatization may be extended by allowing the children to ask the Magi any questions they might have or by asking the children questions that require a longer response.

ADVENT JOURNEY

by Mabelle McGuire

When I traveled from Nazareth to Jerusalem, I kept thinking of Mary's journey to Bethlehem which was eight miles farther. What is just a pleasant drive today was a long trip then. But Joseph and his wife had to go because of a nation-wide census that Rome had declared in order to get more taxes from the people.

As it was almost time for Mary to have her baby, she would no doubt have preferred to stay at home, but Roman soldiers were in Galilee as elsewhere. On the Sabbath, the day when Jews could not travel, they would make camp and rest. Surely the journey would not take more than six days. And she could ride their donkey.

In the puzzle there are three isolated letters that spell the name of the One who upheld them and kept them safe from bandits and jackals while traveling through the open country. In this manner "Advent" started with a journey.

B	B	L	A	N	K	E	T	Y	W	C
A	A	E	D	O	O	F	E	A	A	E
G	B	F	T	A	X	K	L	M	T	N
N	Y	I	T	H	N	K	P	H	E	S
I	E	N	G	O	L	H	T	O	R	U
L	N	K	D	A	P	E	D	A	Y	S
D	R	I	D	E	R	A	H	D	R	D
D	U	T	S	A	I	N	N	E	A	R
A	O	O	Z	S	I	X	S	O	M	O
W	J	A	C	K	A	L	L	E	E	C
S	N	S	D	N	A	B	R	E	A	D
M	O	N	E	Y	S	L	O	O	T	T

List: BAG, BANDS, BETHLEHEM, BLANKET, BREAD, CAMP, CENSUS, CORD, DAYS, DONKEY, FOOD, INN, JACKAL, JOSEPH, JOURNEY, KIT, KNIFE, LOAD, MARY, MEAT, MONEY, NAZARETH, PAD, PAN, POT, RIDE, SEAT, SIX, SWADDLING, TOOLS, TAX, WALK, WATER.

The Long
Long Christmas List

by Beverly McCall

This is a Christmas puppet skit for two muppets or hand puppets, in this case, named Molly and Ollie. Children comprise an audience, seated on the floor in front of the puppet stage.

MOLLY: (Comes on stage, singing) Joy to the world! The Lord has come! Let earth receive her King!

OLLIE: (Back stage) Molly! Molly! Where are you?

MOLLY: Up here, Ollie. Come on upstairs. All the kids are here to practice our Christmas program.

OLLIE: Oh, Molly. We can't practice *now*. We just can't.

MOLLY: We can't practice? Why not?

OLLIE: I'm too busy!

MOLLY: But, Ollie. Everybody's here! See? Hi, everybody!

(Children respond: Hi, Molly! Hi, Ollie!)

OLLIE: (slowly and sadly) Hi, kids.

MOLLY: Ollie, you sound down-hearted! What's wrong?

OLLIE: W e l l ... I've got this long, long Christmas list (pulls up a very long paper). And I don't have any money for presents. And I don't have any time to make anything either.

MOLLY: Wow, that sure is a long list!

OLLIE: I've just about given up on being able to give something to everyone.

MOLLY: Let's see who is on your list.

OLLIE: Well, I've got Mom and Dad and you and Grandma. Then there's Grandpa and my church school teacher.

MOLLY: Don't forget Bobby's name.

OLLIE: Yes, I know. I know. And Uncle Don and Uncle Dan and Aunt Ann and Susy and Cousin Mike and Cindy, and it just goes on and on and on and on. Oh, me, what can I do?

MOLLY: Oh, Ollie, I wish I could cheer you up. Christmas should be a happy time. I don't think Jesus wants you to be sad for his birthday.

OLLIE: I know. I know. I'm trying to be happy for Christmas but I just can't stop worrying about this long list.

MOLLY: Oh, Ollie, you know what? I've noticed something! Happy people sing a lot. Music can make us happy. Let's listen a minute while the kids practice the Christmas program song.

OLLIE: O.K. Maybe that will make me feel better.

MOLLY: All right, everybody. Let's all sing "Joy to the World!"

(Children and puppets sing "Joy to the World!")

MOLLY: How do you feel now, Ollie?

OLLIE: W e l l ...a little better, but I still have this list! The song didn't make the list go away.

MOLLY: So I see! Hey, smile. I think I have another idea!

OLLIE: An idea! Oh, good. I sure need help.

MOLLY: Yes, I think I have a good way to remember everyone at Christmas and to share your own self. After all, that's what God did the first Christmas when He shared His son, Jesus with the world.

OLLIE: Let's hear it then.

MOLLY: Well, why don't you think of something special you could do for each person on your list and then make a gift certificate telling each person what you will do for them.

OLLIE: I'm not sure what you mean.

MOLLY: Well, how about the first person on your list — Dad! Why don't you tell him you will shovel snow for him free during vacation?

OLLIE: Oh, I get it. I write on paper, "Good for free snow shoveling during Christmas vacation." Then I wrap it up in a box and give it to Dad for Christmas?

MOLLY: Yes, yes, that's right.

OLLIE: (excited) Oh, Molly! This is great! I'm going to get some wrapping paper and get busy. (exits)

MOLLY: Ollie, what about the Christmas program?

OLLIE: (Comes on stage again, with ribbon on head, paper in mouth) I've got time to practice now and I feel great! Let's see. I think I'll promise to visit Grandma once a week. And, I'll give Bobby a gift certificate that says, "I'll pick up your toys for your every Saturday." And I'll tell Cousin Mike he can spend one week end here with me. Wow! (Ollie starts to sing "Joy to the World!" and everyone joins in singing, and he exits.)

End.

THE SHEPHERD BOY

by Ruby Peregrine

The air was crisp and still. Scarcely a sound could be heard save for an occasional bleating of a lamb. Far up the hillside a tiny fire flickered, throwing a light upon the forms that hovered over it. The men were sturdy shepherds dressed in coats of loosely woven cloth. They were weary from the long journey with their sheep. Only Dan, a lad of ten, seemed to be awake to the beauties of the night about him. He sat gazing into the heavens as he strummed his harp. Then in the spirit of worship he began to sing the old shepherd psalm. One of the shepherds roused himself and exclaimed, in a scolding voice, "Dan, why do you play that harp? Don't you know that you disturb me?"

"I'm sorry if you are annoyed," Dan replied, "I shall go over on the other side of the hill by myself."

"But why do you play that harp anyway?" the old shepherd replied, not satisfied just to have Dan go away.

Dan knew that the old man would laugh at him. He did not understand his dreams, but slowly he answered him, "I wish to learn to play as well as David of old. I want to make my harp strings ring out beautiful music. Perhaps, someday, I might play for a king, as did David."

The old shepherd laughed loudly, rousing the other shepherds. "You, lad, learn to play as well as David? David was a musician. Not even a babe could stand to hear you play. If that is why you strum that harp you might as well quit now."

The other shepherds began to take notice of the talk about the harp. "There is no king of Israel now, Dan," Isaac said, "How could you ever play for a king?"

"Oh, I have heard the Scriptures read, and I have heard stories from my mother. There is a new king coming someday to reign over David's kingdom. I want to learn to play beautiful music so I can play for the Baby Prince." Dan went off a little way from the others and sat down and began to softly strum his harp.

"I am going to sleep for a little while. Will you watch over my sheep, Dan?" called Isaac as he stretched out on the ground in front of the fire.

"Yes, I will, Isaac," called back Dan, cheerfully.

Then the other shepherds began to prepare for a nap. They, too, wanted Dan to watch their sheep. Even old Levi, who had scolded him called rather sternly, "And watch my flock, too, lad."

Dan replied cheerfully that he would care for Levi's sheep. Surely the old man meant no harm when he scolded him. As soon as he thought the men were asleep he began to strum his harp and sing the 'Shepherd's Psalm'. Suddenly he stopped! There seemed to be music in the air. A strange song! A new song seemed to charm him as he sat and listened. It grew nearer and nearer. He suddenly jumped to his feet.

"What is this I hear?" he cried, as he ran toward the shepherds. They, too, were startled. They heard voices singing, as though they were angels. "Glory to God in the highest, and on earth peace among men with whom he is pleased."

The shepherds were afraid and fell on the ground trembling. "Don't be afraid," an angel said to them, "for behold I bring you good news of great joy which shall come to all people; for to you is born this day in the city of David a Savior, who is Christ the Lord. And this will be a sign for you: you will find a babe wrapped in swaddling cloths and lying in a manger."

Then there was a multitude of angels singing 'Glory to God in the highest, and on earth peace among men in whom he is pleased.'

The shepherds listened with awe. Their vision touched them deeply. They sat quietly for a moment. Then the youngest of them said eagerly, "Let's go to Bethlehem and see what this is all about."

"Benjamin is right," Matthew replied, "we must go to Bethlehem. It may be that a king of Israel is born, for something wonderful has happened."

The shepherds arose and started down the hillside. Dan quickly picked up his harp, tucked it under his arm and followed after the men. "Are you going, Dan?" Levi asked with a sharp voice.

"That I am, Levi," Dan answered excitedly.

"Then why do you take your harp?"

Dan hesitated.   He did not know that Levi saw him tuck his harp under his arm. He knew that he would make fun of him, but he smiled at the old man and said rather slowly, "I thought, perhaps, I might play for the Babe in the manger, and if he were the king of Israel. . ."

The old shepherd interrupted him. "You dreamer, lad. Lay your harp down if you are going with us."

"Aye, no," begged Dan, "I pray you don't scold me. I want to take my harp."

The old shepherd went on for he feared that he couldn't keep up with the others. But he called back to Dan, "If you tarry, you will be left behind."

Dan did not care if the other went before him. It was almost dawn and he could see them as they went down the hill. He stopped to tune the strings on his harp. Then he again tucked it under his arm and started to run toward Bethlehem. He had not gone far when he heard a faint cry. Dan knew that it was the cry of a lamb lost or in pain. He picked up his staff and rod. He could not pass by a sheep in need of a shepherd's help. He groped his way along the edge of a deep ditch. He paused and gave a call: — "ta-ra-ra, ro,oo, oo, oo." The cry of the lamb made Dan's heart beat faster. It was suffering and needed help. Down at the bottom of the ditch he found it. It was scared and scratched. He took it in his arms and hurried toward the little fire. He sat down to care for it.

"Ah, you are one of Levi's fairest flock," he said. "I will annoint your head with oil and perhaps you will feel better."

He took care of the bruises, gave the lamb a drink of water from his jug, put a cloak down for it, near the fire, and turned to follow the others. They were now out of sight but he was fleet of foot and could catch them before they got to the gate of the city. But as he started to leave the lamb, still frightened, it called after him. That stirred the others and they huddled together and gave frightened cries. Dan stopped and thought of the sheep. The others had forgotten that a shepherd never leaves his sheep alone. "Poor little lambs," said Dan as some of the small ones crowded around him, "I will not leave you."

Dan looked longingly toward Bethlehem. Then he stirred the fire, sat down and picked up his harp. His fingers strummed the strings as he sat there and dreamed of the vision of the night before. He seemed to hear the angel song over and over in his mind — the song of 'peace on earth and good will to all.' How he wished that he could be in Bethlehem. He would not get to play for the Babe in the manger. His dream of playing for a King would not come true. It had all been a dream — but what a dream it was! He could hear that song — and began to sing as his fingers strummed the strings.

"I did not get to go and see the new born King," he said to himself, "but I will learn to sing the angels' song: Glory to God in the highest . . ."

An hour or more passed by as Dan sat on the hillside strumming his harp and singing. Up the hill came the other shepherds. They walked silently. None of them wished to talk. Then they paused. "Listen," said old man Levi, "I hear the angels' song. They have come back."

"It is just Dan, playing his harp and singing."

"Dan, nothing," answered Levi, "it is the angels' song."

All the shepherds quickened their pace but the old man passed them all. When he got close to the place where they had camped for the night he stopped short. When he saw Dan, there was a funny lump in his throat. He listened for a moment and then spoke, "Dan," he said.

"Yes, Levi."

"Would you play for me?"

Through the crisp morning air rang the music of "Glory to God in the highest."

FIRST CHRISTMAS

by Mabelle McGuire

You are invited to play a word game that tells the story of the first Christmas. Draw a line around each of the words found in the list. Four isolated letters spell the word that means devotion and affection. There was much of it in the humble stable on that night of joy.

M	D	R	E	H	P	E	H	S	D	J
A	E	G	N	I	N	R	A	W	O	E
R	N	H	T	E	R	A	Z	A	N	S
Y	D	I	E	P	L	G	N	I	K	U
J	L	O	M	L	Y	C	O	G	E	S
O	O	O	G	A	H	G	A	A	Y	T
S	T	U	H	O	L	T	E	M	E	A
E	N	F	R	A	L	I	E	V	E	B
P	O	U	I	N	Y	D	N	B	L	L
H	S	A	N	G	E	L	S	N	F	E
R	E	H	T	O	M	Y	R	R	H	E

List: ANGELS, ANIMAL, BETHLEHEM, CAMEL, CHORUS, DONKEY, EGYPT, FLEE, GIFT, GOD, GOLD, HAY, HOLY, INN, JESUS, JOSEPH, JOURNEY, KING, MAGI, MARY, MOTHER, MYRRH, NAZARETH, SHEPHERD, SON, STABLE, WARNING.

Answer: The hidden word is LOVE.

Identifying Christmas Concepts

by Jill R. Edens

ACTIVITY I

Materials needed: old Christmas cards, magazines, catalogues, mural paper, construction paper, glue.

During the Christmas season we especially remember many of our Christian concepts. "Joy," "peace," "the nativity," "gifts," "new birth" all find their place in the Christmas celebrations. While our young people become conscious of many or all of the concepts during this season, they may find their experiences are one huge jumble that needs to be sorted out. One way to facilitate this sorting-out process is to use old Christmas cards or pictures from magazines or catalogues to help illustrate the Christian concepts.

Have the children bring in as many old Christmas cards as they can. Put the collection on a table in the middle of the room. From large pieces of colored construction paper make cards and print one concept on each card in large letters; i.e. JOY, PEACE, GIFTS, NATIVITY. Ask the children what they think each means. When you are satisfied that they understand, place the concept cards on the floor around the table. Now let the children sort through the pile of Christmas cards and put each card under the appropriate concept. When all have been sorted, ask the children if they found any that didn't fit under any of the concept categories. If they did, let them think up some new categories for these cards.

This project can easily be turned into a bulletin board display by attaching the concept cards to a large piece of mural paper and allowing the children to paste the Christmas cards that best illustrate each concept under the appropriate word. Shiny Christmas garlands make a festive trimming for your new bulletin board!

ACTIVITY II

Another way to help children identify Christmas concepts is to build collages with old Christmas cards. For this project you will need: old Christmas cards, magazine, catalogues, glue, colored construction paper, scissors, crayons or colored pens, colored chalk.

Begin by having several concepts "joy," "peace," "nativity," written on a chalkboard (red and green chalk will help brighten the room!). Ask the children to think of additional concepts. When the list has been completed, let each child choose his/her favorite concept and write it across the top of his/her paper in crayon or colored marking pen. Large pieces of colored construction paper work well with this project. The children may then be invited to sort through the pile of old Christmas cards, magazines, catalogues, etc. until they find the pictures that best illustrate their concepts. Using the pictures, they may cut, arrange, and experiment until they arrive at the most effective design for their collages. When all the pictures are in place exactly as they want them, they may paste everything to their papers.

It is important that the members of the class have a chance to discuss their collages after they are finished. Children should be encouraged to share their thoughts on why they chose the pictures and the arrangement that they did, although they should not be forced to share.

ANGEL

by Linda S. Davidson

Materials needed: various colors of construction paper, stapler, scissors, black felt-tipped pens.

For this angel make the three pattern pieces using the illustration here. Have several patterns available for the children to trace. The three pieces can each be cut from different colors or all from the same color; however we suggest that the front piece with the head be of white paper so the face will show up well.

Have each child cut one of each of the three pattern pieces. Now take the body piece and wrap it around to form a cone. Holding it in place, put the wing piece behind it and staple the two together. After the child draws a face on the front piece, staple it to the front of the body. The expressions the children draw on the faces will delight everyone!

CHRISTMAS TREE BULLETIN BOARD

by Linda S. Davidson

Here is an activity project for Advent which will produce not only a pretty bulletin board but perhaps get your class to think about the real meaning of Christmas. Mount a large construction paper tree on a bulletin board. On each of the four Sundays of Advent, have each child put up one paper ornament, which is cut out on a fold, so it opens up after being cut out. Provide patterns of ornaments for the children to trace on construction paper. On the folded ornament each child will write "How I Am Going to Be Helpful Until Christmas", or "What Christmas Means to Me", or "Why Jesus Came at Christmas", or "What Gift Would I give to Jesus" or whatever idea you wish them to think about. As they pin up their ornaments each week discuss their answers and try to get them to realize the true meaning of Christmas.

Christmas Cards

by Linda S. Davidson

Materials needed: several colors of construction paper, patterns, glue, scissors, crayons, pens.

Children enjoy making Christmas cards for their parents or a special friend. We have all seen traditional silhouette cards of black on white. But at Christmas so many combinations are pretty. Cut silhouettes from most any color construction paper and then mount them on a contrasting color. The possibilities are infinite.

For patterns, use very simple cut-outs so the children will not have to work with intricate designs for cutting. One of the best places to find basic patterns is a children's coloring book. Make some patterns for your class from construction paper or something heavier and have those ready at class time for the children to trace.

Have the children select a pattern and color of paper for their cut-out. They should trace the pattern and then cut it out. Let them then pick another color of paper on which they will glue the cut-out. They can fold this paper once or twice depending on the size of the silhouette. Finally with a crayon or pen   they should write their Christmas message inside and sign the card. See how pleased they will be with their very own hand-made Christmas cards!

A variation of this would be to spatter paint over the pattern for an interesting effect. Additional material you will need for this are: an old toothbrush, newspapers, poster paint or colored ink. After selecting a pattern, fold the card in half and cover what will be the back of the card with newspaper so only the front will be spray painted. Place the pattern where desired on the card and spray thin poster paint or colored ink over the card using an old toothbrush. Rub your thumb across the toothbrush to create the spray effect. When dry remove the pattern piece. Then finish the inside as above to complete the card.

Christmas Ornament

By Brenda Alexander

Materials needed: clear plastic lids from margarine tubs, old Christmas cards, glue, paper punch, and scraps of yarn or ribbon approximately six inches in length.

This is a quick and easy ornament for young children to make during the holidays. Ask the children to bring margarine lids and old Christmas cards from home. This will save you a lot of time tracking down these materials.

Place the margarine lids over a picture on a Christmas card. Trace around the outside and then cut to a size that will fit on the inside of the lid. Glue the picture on the inside of the lid with the desired side facing out. Cover the back of the card with a circle cut the same size from construction paper, if desired. When completely dry, punch a hole in the lid at the top of the picture, string with yarn or ribbon and hang on the Christmas tree. Glitter may be added for a special effect.

Materials needed: paper nut cups; 5, 7, or 9 ounce paper cups; 2-inch styrofoam balls; large-headed colored pins, map tacks or sequins; cotton balls; scraps of rick-rack, braid, trim and yarn; glue; and a box.

Paper Cup Crèche

by Linda S. Davidson

The purpose of this activity is to help young children become aware of and familiar with the characters in a creche scene. Begin by briefly discussing each figure in the creche, holding up samples of each. Then have the children make one character a piece with the above materials.

Paper cups may seem an unusual material to make figures from, but do try this! Precious little characters can be created by children from these materials.

Begin with a paper cup turned upside down. Glue a nut cup upside down on top of the large cup. On top of the nut cup, glue a styrofoam ball. This will complete the head, neck and body. (For added interest paint the styrofoam balls in flesh tones before class.) Add two pins for eyes, and depending on the character the child is creating, glue on yarn or cotton balls for hair, or sliced-off cups for crowns. Crowns should be pre-cut and various trims may be added for decoration.

The baby Jesus can be represented by a small styrofoam ball resting on cotton balls in a cut-off cup manger. Encourage the young artists' creativity by giving assistance only when the children ask for it.

After the children complete their figures have a box or other material ready to serve as a stable. Introduce the newly-created characters by inviting the children, one at a time, to come forward and tell about each. These figures may then serve as visuals for a brief telling of the Christmas story after which each child should be able to identify all of the characters.

Wreaths

by Linda S. Davidson

Materials needed: cardboard, various sizes and shapes of macaroni, glue, silver and gold spray paint, ribbon, pipe cleaners or wire.

This project will take some time, so you should allow 2-3 Sundays to work on it. To begin take some cardboard and cut out the wreaths (about 8 inches in diameter is a good size). Use an X-acto knife or razor blade for cutting. Scissors do not work well on cardboard! Have a large selection of macaroni available. Have the class glue macaroni to the cardboard wreaths, as close together as possible. Let them dry.

Next spray paint the wreaths when they are completely dry. Use lots of newspaper to protect the surrounding area or spray them in a box. We would advise an adult doing this step.

Make bows from the ribbon. Loop a pipe cleaner or wire through the center of the bow, making sure it does not show. Make a small hole in the wreath and push the pipe cleaner through it. Straighten the bow and twist the pipe cleaner tight on the back of the wreath. Form a circle with the pipe cleaner or wire for a loop on the back by which to hang the wreath. These are most attractive when finished and anyone would be delighted to receive one from a child!

SNOWMAN

by Linda S. Davidson

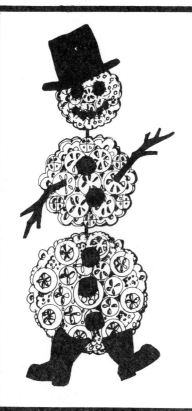

You will need: Doilies, glue, thread or string, construction paper, scissors.

To make a cute snowman mobile, take three doilies and add features and details as desired. Glue and thread or string between the three doilies and hang.

For a cottonball snowman you will need: cotton balls, construction paper, glue.

Cut a snowman from construction paper. With glue, completely cover him with cotton balls or even miniature marshmallows! Cut features, hat, buttons, etc. from construction paper and glue on top of the cotton balls. Children will love these fluffy guys. If you use miniature marshmallows, plan for plenty of extras as some will be eaten!

Wise Men

by Linda S. Davidson

Materials needed: construction paper of various colors including white, scissors, black felt-tipped pens.

To make these cute characters, begin with the body. Cut paper in squares. Fold each peice in half. Cut a slit to the right and left hand sides of the top edges. Next for the heads draw and cut out rectangles of white paper — half as wide as the colored squares. Make two slits in each at the bottom edge. Then using a black pen, draw on faces on the white paper. Mount the faces by pushing the slits at the bottom of the ractangles over the slits at the top of the squares.

Crèche Scene

by Linda S. Davidson

Materials needed: construction paper in blue, brown and white, glue, scissors, pencils, glitter, if desired.

This is a simple project for pre-school children to make during Advent. Before class make simple patterns as seen in the illustration of Mary, Joseph, and the baby Jesus. To begin the project, let each child trace these simple figures on white paper and then cut them out. Children of this age do not cut well, so just let them do their best. Exactness in this project is not necessary as you can see! After each child has his/her three figures, give out large 12 x 18 inch pieces of blue construction paper. Have the children glue Mary, Joseph and the baby Jesus on the paper. Then let them cut three strips from brown paper. Glue these three strips around the figures, forming the stable. If desired, you can offer glitter to be glued on the figures. As they work on these, repeat the names of the characters in the creche scene so they will become familiar with them.

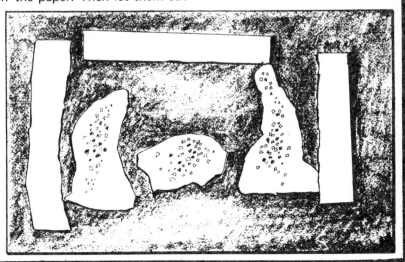

Christmas Banners

by Linda S. Davidson

Materials needed: burlap, felt, scraps of fabric, scissors, glue, bits of trims, ribbon, old jewelry, etc.

To create some Christmas banners, try to have available a great variety of scrap fabric, the more textures and colors, the better. Call a few mothers and ask them to send old scraps of material to church with their young people. A class can work on one large banner together or each youth can make his/her own smaller one. Suggest a specific theme, such as a creche scene with Mary, Joseph and the baby, or perhaps a manger scene as in our illustration, using various wooly fabrics for the animals with maybe some straw around the manger, or try the three Wise Men, with rich velvets and satins for their robes. Or just let the young people create their own thing!

Junior and senior highers will be able to make more detailed and intricate designs than younger children, although the same idea could be used with lower grade levels. But junior and senior high young people can really produce lovely works of art when given the opportunity to use their creativity. When complete, the banners can be displayed around the church for all to enjoy or take them to shut-ins to brighten their rooms or use them for Christmas gifts.

Christmas Card Basket

by Linda S. Davidson

Materials needed for one basket: 14 old Christmas cards, punch, stapler, yarn.

This basket makes a delightful gift either filled with holiday cookies or some other hand-crafted creation. Cut 12 old Christmas cards to the shape seen in the illustration; the bottom of each card measures 2¼ inches, the widest part 3½ inches, and the highest point 4¼ inches. Staple two cards together at the bottom, making six pairs with wrong sides together. Punch four holes down each side and three across each bottom of these six pairs. For the bottom of the basket cut two cards in a 4-inch hexagon. Staple together the two pieces, wrong sides together again, and then punch twelve holes around it, three along each edge. With yarn lace together the six sides and bottom piece. Then fill it with cookies, candy or whatever and there is a lovely Christmas gift that a child made him/herself.

Simple Advent banners became the basis for four lessons during Advent: Hope, Peace, Love, and Joy. Each Sunday we added a symbol to our banners and built a lesson around its meaning. The banners were made by all classes preschool through sixth grade. In the preschool classes more complicated pieces were first glued together by the teacher and the whole figure was then placed on the banner by the child and decorated. The Advent banners and lessons could easily be adapted to learning centers or workshops. All the banners were used to decorate the sanctuary for the Christmas Eve service. On the back of each banner we attached a sheet explaining the meaning of the various colors and symbols so that the banner would become a treasured part of each family's Christmas decorations and each year would serve as a reminder of the meaning of Advent. The banners measured 9 x 23 inches. One inch at the top was folded over and the edge glued to the back so that a dowel could be inserted for hanging.

MEANING OF THE ADVENT BANNER
(attached to the back of the banners)

HOPE — (star) The wisemen followed the star in the hope they would find the Christ (Matthew 2:1-8)

PEACE - (Mary, Joseph, Jesus) Finding the babe in the manger, the wisemen and shepherds found the peace that Christ's love brings to each of us (Luke 2:1-20)

LOVE — (wisemen) They gave their most treasured gifts to Jesus, so also we bring him our most treasured gift — ourselves (Matthew 2:1-11)

JOY — (angels) The real joy of Christmas is in sharing its message and meaning with others as did the angels and shepherds (Luke 2:10)

MEANING OF COLORS AND SHAPES IN THE BANNER

Gold — The richness and abundance of God's love (background).

Light green — Peace, new life in Christ (triangle, tree-shaped).

Purple — Royalty, also the color of preparation (wisemen).

Triangle — Christmas tree, God's eternal love (tree)

Advent Banners: Lasting Symbols of God's Love

by Colleen Britton

Christmas Balls

by   Linda S. Davidson

Materials needed: scraps of fabric, 3-inch styrofoam balls, scissors, table knives, ribbon.

These lovely balls are very simple for older children (4th grade and up) to make and when complete, give a quilted effect.

Let each class member cut fabric scraps into very small pieces. Take one piece and gently push it into the ball with the table knife. Put the knife just inside the edge of the fabric and stick it into the ball. After everyone has done a couple pieces they will develop a feel for how it is done. Cover the entire ball with little scraps, either in a pattern or randomly. When completely covered, tie ribbon around it to hang on a tree. Everyone will be delighted with their "quilted" Christmas balls.

Stained Glass Windows For Christmas

by Anne Neufeld Rupp

What are you doing for Christmas? In your classroom, I mean. Sometimes we culminate everything during the season with the children's annual program, or the something "special" which occurs in the class on the Sunday prior to the Nativity event. What about a process which could carry your class from Thanksgiving, through Advent, to Christmas?

What am I suggesting? I am talking about a mural painted on glass. If you are fortunate enough to have a classroom on the first floor, your window is ideally suited. If not, you may be able to find a large sheet of glass, or a storm door window which could be used.

What will you paint? Take a look at your class. What does this season mean to them? How is Thanksgiving related to Advent and Christmas? How is this related to the quarter's material which they have just studied? As you and the class discuss and share, you will come to some convictions and beliefs about what you want to express on glass. You may want to create one picture to which each child contributes a part, or you may want to make a series of motifs or symbols.

How do you go about the process? Cut newsprint the size of your window or glass. Tape together if necessary. The class now draws the scenes or symbols it wishes to portray. Tape the paper to the outside of the window with the sketched picture facing you. Various children may paint various parts of the scene with tempera. You will want to do some experimenting with the tempera paint. Some types or colors crack or run more easily than others. For a "leaded" effect on your "stained" glass window, use a broad felt tip pen in black.

If you used a window, you may want to work out a lighting effect so that passers-by may see your scene after dusk.

Tree Ornaments

by Linda S. Davidson

Materials needed: foil (heavy craft or decorator kind) or aluminum pie plates, pencils, scissors, thread or yarn, patterns, punch.

For shiny tree ornaments that will glisten and sparkle from the tree lights, try using heavy craft foil or aluminum pie plates. You can use any simple Christmas shape, but these make especially pretty stars.

Make the patterns ahead of time for your class. A child's Christmas coloring book will offer a wide selection of patterns from which to pick. Do not use complicated designs, just simple, easy-to-cut ones. Have the class trace a pattern on a pie plate or foil and then cut it out. Punch a hole at the top. Using thread, fishing line or yarn, tie a large loop through the hole so the ornament can be hung. Glitter may be added if desired. Of course, construction paper can be used instead.

For a 3-dimensional ornament, cut two shapes exactly alike. Cut a slit on one from the top to half way down the middle. On the second one, slit it from the bottom to half way up. Then slide the two together.

Christmas Bells

by Linda S. Davidson

Materials needed: paper cups, aluminum foil, ribbon, small Christmas bells.

For centuries bells have been used to express joy and to announce important events. Bells appeared in Christian churches during the sixth century and announced the birthday of Jesus on Christmas Eve or Christmas Day. Their use has grown through the ages until today we hear chimes, bells, and carillons weeks before Christmas to announce the coming of this joyful event.

This simple activity is one that preschoolers will enjoy and it might help them catch the Christmas spirit and mood. First give each child a paper cup. (It would be advisable if you put holes in the bottom of each one before class time.) Give a square of aluminum foil to each child and have him/her crumple it around the cup. Thread one or two bells on a piece of ribbon. Poke the ribbon with the bells through the hole in the bottom of the cup. (The cup is held upside down with the bells hanging on the inside.) Make a loop with the ribbon and tie it so the child can hang it on a tree or doorhandle. You might all jingle your bells together to make a joyful noise!

Youth Activities

I WAS THERE

by Robert G. Davidson

Advent is a time each year when we should rethink the meaning and place of Jesus in our world and our personal lives. People think of and see Jesus in many different ways. This is true today just as it was on that night so many years ago when he was born and during his life. To stimulate this rethinking and to help young people prepare for Christmas, the following four outlines for celebration services centering on the theme I WAS THERE, may be helpful.

Because candles play an important role in Advent, the services should center around the lighting of one candle each week. They are visible symbols of the coming of the Christmas event. Invite one or two young people to prepare a statement on one of the themes. Questions they might consider while writing their statements are: If you were alive two thousand years ago at the birth of Jesus, how would you have felt about his birth? What would have been your thoughts and reactions? How would you have shared this birth with your family and friends? With the whole world? The young people should use their imaginations and creativity in developing their individual statements. Each service may be developed differently depending on the time allotted and the creativity of the group.

The First Sunday of Advent
Scripture Reading: Luke 2:8-20

I WAS THERE! *I was one of the shepherds at the stable that night when Jesus was born. I would like to share with you what I saw that night and the feelings I felt. There was a soft breeze in the night air but I knew a mighty new force had come into the world.*

The Second Sunday of Advent
Scripture Reading: Matthew 2:1-12

I WAS THERE! *I was one of the Wise Men and I want to tell you why I went to see the child Jesus and why I took him a gift. I would like to share my thoughts as I stood there in that stable, which the star had led us to. There was a feeling of mystery in the silence of that night.*

The Third Sunday of Advent
Scripture Reading: Luke 2:1-7

I WAS THERE! *I was the inn keeper who said, "No! There's no room for you in my inn." I would like to tell you what happened later that night and how my life has never been the same. God was there that night and He affected my life and the lives of everyone else who was there.*

The Fourth Sunday of Advent
Scripture Reading: John 1:1-18

I WAS THERE! *I was young then, that night at the inn in Bethlehem, some thirty years ago. I just happened to be at the inn that glorious night. I would like to recall that night for you, but also I would like to share with you the Good News that Jesus brought to each of us as he shared his life with us — his reaching out, his caring, his love. I would also like to share with you now how the story ended - or did it end there?*

The Nativity: YOU ARE THERE

by Robert G. Davidson

Each year the Christmas stories from Matthew and Luke are read in church services everywhere. We hear about Mary, Joseph, King Herod, the Wise Men from the East, and the shepherds. These persons lived so long ago, but as the story is told and retold they become very contemporary people. The purpose of this program is to gain a better understanding of these biblical persons, how they thought and felt about the nativity, and how we might feel if we were actively involved in the Christmas event today.

Explain to the young people that they are to try to place themselves in the time that Jesus was born and to take on the role of the person or persons they are reading about. From the biblical passages ask them to create a whole story. When the assignment is clear, divide the group into three small study groups, and assign one of the following passages to each:

Group 1 — Matthew 1:18-25.
Characters to be developed in this passage are Joseph and Mary *(family)*.

Group 2 — Matthew 2:1-12.
Characters to be developed in this passage are Herod the King *(power)* and the Wise Men from the East *(influence and knowledge)*.

Group 3 — Luke 2:8-20.
Characters to be developed are the shepherds *(common people)*.

The following questions might be helpful in developing the characters:

1. How did this person feel about the birth of Jesus?

2. How would the birth of the Son of God affect the life of this person?

3. If this really was the Son of God, would this person want to change his or her past?

4. How would this person's life change in the future?

Give each group time to develop its character(s) into a short story or play. The words in italics may be helpful in developing certain aspects of their characters. Each group may begin by reading the biblical passage and then making its presentation to the other groups. Follow the presentation with discussion and the question: How would you feel if Jesus were born today and you were one of the key characters in the story? Select one character and tell how you think you would react.

COLLEGE PROGRAM

HOME for the HOLIDAYS

by Robert G. Davidson

Christmas is a time for renewing friendships, for catching up, for remembering. This is especially true for our young people who have been away at college. In the coming weeks we will find them looking for a place to gather. If we are alert to their needs, the church will take this opportunity to sponsor an open house at the home either of a willing parent or of the minister, if he or she wishes. One of the evenings between Christmas and New Year's might be a good time to share a happening.

There need be no specific program planned; the shared conversation will fill the evening and build a memory. A bowl of hot spiced wassail punch and trays of holiday cookies will be all that is needed to create an atmosphere of fellowship.

In this holiday season let us not miss any opportunity to let our young people know that we have missed them and are glad they are home with us again. Such gatherings help them realize that they are a continuing part of our local church community.

WHAT IS GOD UP TO?

by Robert G. Davidson

Christmas is coming — a time when we celebrate the birth of Jesus. We all enjoy the excitement of Christmas and look forward to it with great expectation. At the same time we seem to question the place of Jesus and even God in the whole event. This program may help young people deal with the serious questions about how the coming of Jesus and what he said and did affects the present world and its future, when considering his central message about the kingdom of God.

Jesus preached one central message through his earthly ministry — "The time has come; the kingdom of God is upon you; repent, and believe in the Gospel" (Mark 1:15). Time and time again Jesus spoke of the kingdom, pointed to its nearness, and called for persons to change their ways and come into a deeper relationship with God.

Nowhere does Jesus define the kingdom of God precisely. He uses metaphors, similes, and parables to describe what the kingdom is like. Possibly it is because he conceived of the kingdom in terms of personal relationships that he refused to define it precisely. A person comes into God's kingdom, not by knowing about it and the rules which might govern it, but by changing his/her present way of living and coming into a closer relationship with God. Only as a person comes personally to trust God does he/she enter the kingdom.

Jesus emphasized in many of his parables and other teachings that the kingdom is a present reality, about to come and that all persons were welcome to enter into it. At the same time, Jesus also seemed to say that the kingdom of God is in the future.

And so, the nature of the kingdom holds together the present and the future. God's kingdom has come in the life of each person, but the present and the future are linked by the moment of personal decision in every individual's life.

Begin the program by writing the words KINGDOM OF GOD on a chalkboard and asking the group what the term means to them. Draw out as many responses as possible. After everyone who wishes has had an opportunity to respond read Jesus' first sermon (Mark 1:14-15) to the group and spend a few minutes discussing what it is saying to people today.

At this point have the group divide into small conversation groups and assign one of the following parables to each group. Have the young people consider three central questions concerning each parable:

• What does the story mean?

• What does it say to you about the Kingdom?

• How would your lives change if you followed the teachings in your everyday living?

Next assign the following parables to small groups:

Matthew 18:23-35
Matthew 13:24-30
Mark 4:26-29
Luke 18:9-14
Mark 4:30-32
Mark 12:28-34

Give the conversation groups about fifteen minutes to study their passages and then have each group present their answer to the three central questions to the entire group. More questions for discussion are:

▪ What is the kingdom of God?

▪ What does it have to do with you and me?

▪ When will it come or is it here and we cannot see or understand it?

▪ Do we really want to be part of the kingdom?

▪ As we celebrate Christmas, the coming of Jesus, should we rethink our commitment of being part of the kingdom?

Conclude the program with the question: Has God already initiated His kingdom through the life, death, and resurrection of Jesus as the Christ, and has He given human persons the responsibility of bringing it into actuality?

JOYOUS SEASON

by Mabelle McGuire

Draw a line around each word in the list below. All of them tie in with this joyous season. Six isolated letters spell the name of the one whose birthday we celebrate.

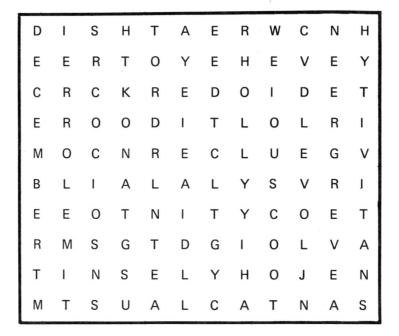

List: BOOK, CANDY, DECEMBER, DECORATION, DISH, DOLL, DOOR, EVE, EVERGREEN, HOLLY, JOY, LIGHT, LOG, LOVE, MISTLETOE, NATIVITY, RED, REINDEER, SANTA CLAUS, TIME, TINSEL, TOY, TREE, TRICYCLE, WREATH, YULE.

Answer: The hidden word is CHRIST.

GOD GAVE TO US

by Robert G. Davidson

Advent is coming and it is again time to rethink the meaning of Jesus in our world and our lives. To stimulate this rethinking, this preparation for Christmas, the following four patterns of celebration services center on the question: "What is the message God gave to us through Jesus?"

Candles play an important role in Advent, and so the services might center around the lighting of one advent candle each week. They are visible symbols of the unifying theme "God Gave To Us!"

Each service may be developed differently depending on the time alloted and the creativity of the worship leader. Music should be included in each service through group singing, background music during meditational times, or solo singing or playing of instruments.

The First Sunday of Advent

Scripture: Philippians 2:1-11

As we light our first Advent candle, let us consider the example which God has given to us in the life and teachings of Jesus. Jesus teaches that we must be concerned about all persons, that we are all equal in the sight of God. He reaches out to the poor and the downtrodden and says we should follow his example.

Jesus shows us how we are to love all persons — until it hurts. He also shows us the all-giving love of God. He touches us and makes us aware of what we might become. Jesus does not say that to follow his example will be easy — it will be hard, there will be difficult decisions and choices to make.

Our first Advent candle reminds us that we have been given an example to live by in Jesus, and ask that God might use us more fully as we endeavor to follow the example of His son.

The Second Sunday of Advent

Scripture: Galatians 5:1

God has given us a new freedom through His son, Jesus, who becomes our example to follow. This freedom allows us to make decisions for ourselves, to choose our relationships, to become the kind of persons we desire to be. Jesus has set the example and we can follow that example or we can turn and go in some other direction — the choice is ours. We can build a relationship with God or we can turn away from God — He has given us this freedom.

As we light our second Advent candle, we offer our individual prayers of thanksgiving to God, and ask that we might use our freedom of choice which He has given so wisely to us.

The Third Sunday of Advent

Scripture: I John 4:7-12

We have an example to follow in Jesus and God has given us the freedom to make choices, and we must assume the responsibility for our actions. We can reach out to others who are in need or we can turn away. We can share our love with other persons and with God or we can deny it. We can search for the deeper meaning and purpose of life or we can struggle in a lonely world.

Let us remember that God has created the world and that His presence is active in the life of all relationships. We should be thankful that He did not create us to be alone, but to have the opportunity for meaningful relationships with other people.

As we light this third Advent candle let us become aware of the ways that we might follow Jesus, our Christ.

The Fourth Sunday of Advent

Scripture: Matthew 5:14-16

We have our example to follow, Jesus. God has lovingly given us freedom of choice. We have been called to be responsible individuals. But, no matter where we are now in our relationships with God, with other persons, we are always being called to be more than we presently are. We are always in the process of becoming a better person, becoming closer to God, becoming a Christian — a Christ follower.

GOD GAVE TO US a world to live in, an example to follow, the freedom of choice, called us to be responsible. And now as we look toward Christmas, how do we respond to the thought: LET US GIVE TO GOD!

As we light our fourth candle let us reflect on our belief in the importance of the coming of Jesus into the world and into our lives, and accept the call to be more than we presently are.

HAPPY BIRTHDAY JESUS!

By Jill R. Edens

The trees are up, the packages are wrapped, the wreaths hung, so why not add a cake and make Jesus' birthday celebration the best ever. The planning for such a party may stimulate some serious thinking about how Jesus might want us to celebrate his birthday and the party itself will surely climax your Christmas celebration.

Objectives:

1. The young people will express their own expectations and feelings concerning Christmas.
2. The young people will review and compare the Christmas stories from the Gospels of Matthew and Luke.
3. The young people will decide with the help of scriptures, what gifts they will give Jesus for his birthday.
4. The class will plan and carry out a birthday celebration for Jesus.

Christmases We Have Celebrated:

Invite the youngsters to complete the following sentences:

1. The best thing about Christmas is . . .
2. The worst thing about Christmas is . . .
3. At Christmas my family and I . . .
4. The most important thing about Christmas is . .
5. Christmas is fun when . . .
6. Christmas makes me think about . . .
7. During the Christmas season we go . . .
8. At Christmas we bake : . .
9. Christmas makes me feel . . .
10. We celebrate Christmas because . . .

Getting the Story Straight:

When class members have finished their sentences, allow plenty of time for sharing and discussion. Continue the lesson with a review of the Christmas story. Divide the class into two groups, one to study Matthew 1:18 — 2:12, and the other to study Luke 2:1-20. Each group should have a discussion leader who can help the group find the answers to the following questions:
1. In what city was Jesus born?
2. Who were Jesus' parents?
3. Which Roman ruler is mentioned in the passage?
4. What special event heralded Jesus' birth?
5. Who came to see the baby Jesus?
6. How did the visitors know they had found him?

Gather the class together and ask the groups to report their answers. Which answers are the same, which are different? Why is it important to read both Matthew and Luke to learn about the Christmas story?

Cause for Celebration or Not?

Looking again at the accounts of Matthew and Luke discuss:
Joseph — Matthew 1:18-20
Wise Men — Matthew 2:1-12
Mary — Luke 2:1-7, 15-20
Shepherds — Luke 2:8-20

1. What are the circumstances of these persons when we first read about them?
2. What happens to change their lives, to give them cause for celebration?
3. The wise men bring gifts to Mary and Jesus. In what way are these "dumb gifts for a baby?" In what way are they entirely appropriate?

Our Own Celebration:

Introduce the idea of having a birthday party for Jesus and ask the young people what they would like to do to celebrate. What kinds of gifts might Jesus want? How might he want this party to be different from other parties?

Divide the class into three groups each to look up one of the following scripture lessons: Matthew 5:3-10; 5:23-24; 5:38-42. In view of these teachings of Jesus, ask the young people what he might want them to do to remember his birthday. Perhaps they will decide to visit a nursing home, wrap gifts for the needy, or write out Christmas messages for shut-ins in the church. Whatever activity they might choose, it should be punctuated with a gala party complete with a birthday cake to celebrate the Advent of the One who made our love for each other possible.

Make The Christmas Tree A Family Tree

by Mary Ward

To prepare for a Christmas celebration that is meanginful and festive, how about looking at the traditional Christmas tree in a new way. This year take the tree symbol seriously and use it as a teaching tool instead of an ornament. Try creating a "Jesus Tree".

Objectives:

1. Young people will share facts about Jesus' ancestory.

2. Young people will create Christmas tree ornaments that represent Jesus' lineage.

Introduce the session by asking young people what they think a family tree is and who might be on their family trees. After a discussion of their family roots, invite the class to look up Matthew 1:1-16. This is the family tree which links Joseph to Abraham. After reading the passage together, assign each member of the class one of the names of the family tree. Provide the class with a concordance, Bible dictionary, Bible story books and books of Christian symbols. Give the children ample time to research the people in the geneology. As an aid, give the following guide:

Name of ancestor _____

Address _____

Occupation _____

Husband or wife's name _____

Children _____

Where in the Bible we can read about this person _____

The most interesting thing I found out about this person _____

My favorite story about this person _____

As an extra assignment, ask all the children to investigate the Jesse Tree by reading Isaiah 11.

After the youth have discovered more about one of the people in the geneology, ask them to think of a symbol, a sign or a word that would remind everyone of this person. With supplies provided, give everyone an opportunity to create a Christmas ornament which tells something about the ancestors. Provide simple styrofoam balls or shapes on which the biblical names can be written. Or using modeling clay, encourage the children to form molds — symbols or letters — and cover them with vaseline, filling them with plaster of paris to be painted when set. Mix up salt-flour-water clay which after being shaped will harden (or can be baked) before being painted. Provide pipe cleaners, fabric, ribbon, glitter and white glue from which shapes and designs can be created.

When everyone has finished, gather around the tree with the ornaments. Read again the geneology in Matthew, stopping when one of the names mentioned has been chosen by one of the class members. Give the student an opportunity to share the information about this ancestor, to show the ornament, and to hang it on the tree. After all the ornaments have been hung, discuss why this is called a Jesus tree. Hang an ornament for Jesus on the top of the tree.

A LIGHT COMES
IN THE WORLD

By Robert G. Davidson

Advent is coming and it is again time to rethink the meaning and place of Jesus in our world and our lives. To stimulate this rethinking, this preparation for Christmas, the following four outlines of celebration services center on the question, "What difference has Jesus made in the purpose of your life and mine?"

Because candles play an important role in Advent, the services center around the lighting of one candle each week. They are visible symbols of the unifying theme "A Light Comes Into the World," based on John 1:1-18. Each service may be developed differently depending on the time allotted and the creativity of the group.

THE FIRST SUNDAY OF ADVENT
Scripture Lessons: Genesis 1:1-5; John 1:1-5

As we light this first Advent candle, let us consider the abundant possibilities God has given to each of us. Let us praise Him for placing us on this beautiful earth with all of its many resources, both natural and human. Let us offer our thanksgiving to God for the creative powers He has given us and ask for guidance, that we might use these resources as they were intended by our Creator.

Let us remember that God has created the world and that His presence is active in the life of all relationships. We are thankful that He did not create us to be alone, but to have meaningful relationships with other people. We praise Him for those relationships.

THE SECOND SUNDAY OF ADVENT
Scripture Lessons: John 1:9-13; Matthew 2:1-2

On this second Sunday of Advent we think of the many things for which we can be thankful. These include the love of persons with whom we worship — our neighbors, our families, our friends. And the love of God who sent His son Jesus into the world, that we might know the meaning of light in our lives.

As we light our second Advent candle, we offer our individual prayers of thanksgiving to God, and ask that He might use us more fully as we endeavor to follow the example of His son.

THE THIRD SUNDAY OF ADVENT
Scripture Lessons: John 1:14-18; I John 4:7-12

On this third Sunday of Advent we turn our thoughts to the message that Jesus brings to us. He reaches out to the poor and the downtrodden. He teaches that we must be concerned about all persons, that we are all equal in the sight of God.

He showed us how we are to love all persons — until it hurts. He showed us the love of God. He taught us the concerns of God. He touched us and made us aware of what we might become. The child born in a manger became the light that leads us to the kingdom of God. Let us think of the ways we might follow Jesus, our Christ.

THE FOURTH SUNDAY OF ADVENT
Scripture Lessons: John 1:1-18; Matthew 5:14-16

On this fourth Sunday of Advent we gather as a community of God's people. He has created a place of majestic beauty to house us; He has sent His light into the world through His Son Jesus, who calls us to become more than we are at present. We can choose not to hear the call because it does not seem important, or we are not ready or we do not have the time. We can also say, "Yes, I will become a light for God."

As we light our fourth candle let us reaffirm our belief in the importance of the coming of Jesus Christ into the world and into our lives. We as the community of God's people will take the message which Jesus brings and share it with others.

SIMPLE GIFTS

by Jill R. Edens

'Tis a gift to be simple
'Tis a gift to be free
'Tis a gift to come down
where you want to be
And when you find a place
that will be just right
'Twill be in the valley of
love and delight.

When true simplicity is gained
We'll bow and we'' bend
and we shant be ashamed
To turn, turn and in our delight
Keep on turning, turning 'till
we come round right.

Shaker Song

Taking its theme from this lovely Shaker song, this junior high worship celebrates the giving of simple gifts.

To prepare for the service, begin a week prior to the time that you plan to hold the service by asking junior highs to make a list of "simple gifts" that have meaning and cost very little, if anything. This list might include a gift certificate for an afternoon of sled riding, a dozen homemade cookies, or a walk home from school.

Next, pass out 3 x 5 cards to the young people and ask them to write their names on them. These will become gift certificates for the next week. The 3 x 5 cards should then be dropped into a hat, mixed up and passed around so that everyone may draw a name. The person named on the card will then be the receiver of a simple gift from the drawer. The gift may be one of those previously listed or it may be especially designed for the receiver.

The service should then proceed the following week with the singing of favorite Christmas carols, "Simple Gifts" and the exchange of gifts and gift certificates.

JESUS

IS

COMING

by Robert G. Davidson

Jesus is coming! Much preparation, a festive season, a grand celebration and there we have it — Christmas. But what does it all mean in the Christian community?

We all enjoy the excitement of Christmas. We look forward to it with expectation. At the same time we seem to question the place of Jesus and even God in the whole event. The purpose of this program is to help young people deal with the serious questions about how the coming of Jesus affected the world of the past, the present, and the future.

Begin the program by asking the young people what Christmas means to them. Record the key words and thoughts on a chalkboard, spending a few moments discussing these ideas. Next, give each person a sheet of paper and ask him/her to respond to the following questions:

• What effect did Jesus' coming have in his day?

• What effect does Jesus' coming have on our world?

• What effect do you think Jesus' coming will have on the world in the future?

After several minutes, ask for volunteers to share their responses with the group. Allow time for discussion and ask: If Jesus had not appeared on this earth, how might it be different? Finally, focus the group's attention on the following question: What is the message God gave to us through Jesus?

In groups of five or six persons each invite young people to discuss which of the following statements comes closest to their understanding of God's message through Jesus:

■ We are responsible persons.

■ We have been given an example to live by.

■ We can make personal decisions.

■ We have a new freedom as human persons.

■ God loves us.

■ We receive continuous support from God.

■ Jesus has come, he continues to be.

■ We have been called to be more than we presently are.

Each group should select a recorder to report its conclusions back to the total group.

A biblical study passage for this program can be found in John 1:1-18.

ADVENT

by Mabelle McGuire

The Bible tells us that God's plan of salvation was to send someone into the world to teach people how to live better. Three isolated letters give the answer to "Whom did He send?" Draw a line around each word and check the list.

List: ADVENT, ANGEL, BETHLEHEM, BIRTH, ELIZABETH, GIFT, GLORY, HOLY, INN, JESUS, JOHN, JOSEPH, KING DAVID, KINSWOMAN, LINEAGE, NAME, RADIANCE, SHEPHERDS, STABLE.

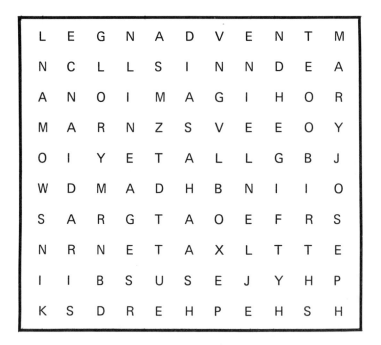

Answer: The hidden word is SON.

For the Love of MONEY

by Jill R. Edens

Scripture lesson: I Timothy 6:10

Christmas is often a painful reminder of how money-rich or money-poor we are in the material world. To help junior highers sort out what they believe money can do for and to them, begin with a discussion based on the following questions followed by the suggested simulation game.

1. Do you have enough money to spend on Christmas this year? If you don't have enough, does that change the way you feel about celebrating Christmas?

2. How did you obtain this money? Did you earn it? How? How long did it take to earn enough to take care of your needs? Or, was the money given to you and did you feel differently about money earned over and against money that was given?

3. Make a list of all the gifts that you will give this Christmas (be sure to keep it secret). Put a star beside the gifts that you feel best about giving. What makes them the best gifts? Were the best gifts necessarily the most expensive ones?

4. Make a second list of all the gifts that you can remember receiving at Christmas. Again, star the gifts that you like the most and give reasons for why they were the best gifts. Did the cost of the gift have anything to do with the way you felt about it?

5. How does money make Christmas better? How can money ruin Christmas?

6. What do you need money for in your everyday living? How can money be "the root of all evil" in your life?

Follow-up the discussion with this simple exercise:

1. Gather everyone around a large table.

2. Give each person a different number of pennies between 0 and 10.

3. Using one finger each person may, in silence, push one penny at a time toward any other person at the table. Continue this procedure for five minutes.

4. For the next five minutes the players may only, in silence, use one finger to take pennies from any other person at the table.

To debrief the players, ask the young people how they felt about pushing pennies to other members of the group while receiving pennies from others. How did they feel about taking pennies and having pennies taken from them? Which part of the exercise did they prefer? What did the exercise tell them about how they feel about money?

SERVICE PROJECT

by Barbara Starkey

Do you have an Advent Wreath-making celebration in your church? If so, turn the gathering of the greens into a service project. Earlier in the season, solicit volunteers to donate greens. Calls to local nurseries should produce an offer of some pines that have overgrown their stay. Church members may also have some trees or bushes they might be willing to offer for pruning.

On the day designated for greens-cutting, plan to have several station wagons, a truck or a van available to haul greens. Ask several parents to accompaany the kids on their task. Assemble saws and axes, along with pruning shears for smaller branches. Meet at the church and travel as a group. While cutting branches or trees, be extremely careful not to damage other plantings. If there is snow on the ground, so much the better. Expect some time to be taken out for snowball fights! While the green are being gathered and transported back to the church, have some other parents prepare a hot chili, cake and cocoa supper   which will be ready upon the return of the group. After the supper, plan for a time of Christmas caroling around a fireplace.

ABOUT THE AUTHORS

ALEXANDER, BRENDA

Brenda Alexander has been an elementary and church school teacher for several years. She is a member of Bay Presbyterian Church, Bay Village, Ohio.

BACON, JANICE

Janice Bacon is the Coordinator of Christian Education for the Hingham Congregational Church, UCC, Hingham, Mass., and a free lance writer.

BRITTON, COLLEEN

Colleen Britton is a free lance writer, art teacher, and church school teacher. She writes church school curriculum and has had several articles published in various national religious publications. She lives in Vacaville, California.

COLLUMS, THELMA

Thelma Collums has been a teacher for many years and is a free lance writer. She resides in Jackson, Mississippi.

DAVIDSON, LINDA

Linda Davidson is on the staff of Educational Ministries, Inc, publisher of this book. Being married to a minister, she taught church school for many years. Now that her husband is a publisher, she edits the monthly craft column in **CHURCH EDUCATOR** and has several other responsibilities in relation to its publication.

DAVIDSON, ROBERT

Robert G. Davidson is an ordained minister in the United Church of Christ. He is editor and publisher of **CHURCH EDUCATOR**, a national monthly publication for Christian educators. It is published by Educational Ministries, Inc., of which he is founder and president.

DAY, N. RAYMOND

N. Raymond Day is a free lance writer with ministerial standing in the Eastern Iowa Association of the United Church of Christ. He is author of FROM PALM SUNDAY TO EASTER and DAVID'S FAITHFULNESS published by Educational Ministries, Inc.

EDENS, JILL

Jill Edens is co-pastor with her husband of the United Church of Chapel Hill, Chapel Hill, North Carolina.

McCALL, BEVERLY

Beverly McCall is a free lance writer and has based many of her articles on experiences she and her husband, a minister, have had in the parish ministry. She resides in Depew, New York.

McGUIRE, MABELLE

Mabelle McGuire is a free lance writer who has had many works published in children's magazines. She lives in Ventura, Calif.

PEREGRINE, RUBY

Ruby Peregrine is Professor Emeritus of Christian Education at Pacific University in Forest Grove, Oregon. She has been an active Christian educator at the local and state levels for many years.

PRIEWE, JANE

Jane Priewe is a free lance writer with articles having appeared in many national educational publications. She resides in Alhambra, California.

RUPP, ANNE NEUFELD

Anne Neufeld Rupp is co-pastor with her husband of the Pleasant Oaks Mennonite Church in Middlebury, Indiana. In addtion to her pastoral duties, she does free lance writing and her articles have appeared in many religious publications.

SCHMIDT, VERNA

Verna Schmidt is a free lance writer having had many articles published in national publications. In addition she is superintendent of the church school of her church in Milwaukee, Wisconsin.

SINCLAIR, JOAN

Joan Sinclair is on the editorial staff of **CHURCH EDUCATOR** and an active member of Lakewood Congregational Church (UCC), Lakewood, Ohio.

STARKEY, BARBARA

Barbara Starkey, a resident of Mansfield, Ohio, is a free lance writer and a regular contributor to **CHURCH EDUCATOR.**

THOMAS, RUDY

Rudy Thomas is the minister of Dover Congregational Church (UCC) in Westlake, Ohio.

WAITE, SHIRLEY

Shirley Pope Waite is a free lance writer, part-time community college instructor, and workshop leader at Christian writers' conferences. She also speaks to women's groups in her area. She lives in Walla Walla, Washington.

WALKER, DELORES

Delores Walker is a free lance writer residing in Walla Walla, Washington.

WARD, ELAINE

Elaine Ward is Director of Children's Ministries at University Park Methodist Church in Dallas, Texas. She also is a photographer and leads workshops in storytelling and does lots of free lance writing.

WARD, MARY

Mary Ward is on the staff of the Family Health Assocation of Cleveland as a professional in family life education. She has spent several years teaching church school at her church in Lakewood, Ohio.